A First Glossary af Hiberno-English

Lis Christensen

A First Glossary af Hiberno-English

Odense University Press 1996

ISK Studiebøger er en serie, der er oprettet med henblik på udgivelse af alment tilgængelige introduktioner til forskningsområder inden for sprog og kommunikation

© Forfatteren, ISK, Odense Universitet og Odense Universitetsforlag 1996
Omslag af Ulla Poulsen Precht
Tegning af Inger Bjerg Poulsen og Laurits Rendboe
Trykt af CAVI
ISBN 87-7838-189-4

CONTENTS

	Page
Abbreviations	6
Preface	7
Select Bibliography	8
Introduction: Sounds, Symbols and Spellings	9
The Two Languages in Ireland	15
Glossary	19
Appendix: A Note on Stage Irishmen and Romantic Clichés	139
Illustrations	141
Authors Quoted	143

ABBREVIATIONS

OE	Old English
OFr.	Old French
ON	Old Norse
abbr.	abbreviation
adj.	adjective
art.	article
cf.	confer
contr.	contracted from
def.	definite
dimin.	diminutive
ed.	editor, edited by
esp.	especially
et al.	*et alia*, and others (esp. of alternative spellings)
etym.	etymology
gen.	genitive
lit.	literally
orig.	originally
pl.	plural
poss.	possessive
pp.	past participle
prob.	probably
pron.	pronoun
spec.	specifically
trans.	translation, translator, translated by
voc.	vocative
–>	refers to a headword

PREFACE

This is a selective word-list designed for those who are approaching, for the first time, texts written in the Irish variety of English.

The vocabulary of Irish-English – or Anglo-Irish, or Hiberno-English – is not always fully understandable to those who are familiar only with Standard English. Many words that may baffle the newcomer are not listed in easily available English dictionaries, however. They may be words of Irish (Gaelic) origin that were and are well-known in Ireland (e.g. *shanachie,* story-teller), or familiar English words that have a different meaning or different associations in Irish contexts (e.g. *guard,* policeman), or words that have dropped out of use in England, but have been preserved in Ireland (e.g. *delft,* crockery). Short of consulting annotated editions or specialist publications, there is little help to be had from written sources for the uninitiated reader, who might like to pick up an Irish novel or leaf through an Irish newspaper.

The present glossary does not claim to be more than 'what every Irish schoolchild knows', but it will hopefully prove to be a helpmeet to general readers and students outside Ireland who have not the leisure or the inclination to embark on more detailed linguistic studies.

Most of the headwords are well known to-day all over Ireland, while some are current only in certain areas. A few older expressions have also been included, plus a handful of names of Government bodies and official organisations, and a minimum of abbreviations. The accompanying quotations illustrate the type of language in which a word will normally be found: colloquial speech typically in fictional or dramatic dialogue or interior monologue (printed in inverted commas), more formal language in poetry (printed with slashes to mark line divisions), etc. Among the authors represented in the examples are many, chiefly from the 20th century, that are often studied outside Ireland (dates are given in the list of Authors Quoted). Quotations from the contemporary press are included as exemplifying present-day idiomatic language familiar to Irish readers.

The glossary does not include Irish (Gaelic) words that are met with notably in writings with a markedly native bias, where they are often italicised: *geocach* (vagrant), *dríocht* (magic), *dúchas* (heredity), et al.; for such words the reader is referred to Irish-English dictionaries. With a few exceptions, the glossary likewise does not list the names of political movements and organisations, which may readily be found in surveys of Irish history.

The inclusion of a word in this glossary should not be taken to mean that it is exclusive to Hiberno-English, or that it may not also occur in Ireland in its customary Standard English sense.

SELECT BIBLIOGRAPHY

Foclóir Póca. English-Irish, Irish-English Dictionary. Dublin: An Gúm, 1986.
The English Dialect Dictionary. Ed. Joseph Wright. 6 vols. 1898-1905; rpt. London: Oxford University Press, 1970.
Bartley, J. O. *Teague, Shenkin and Sawney. Being an historical study of the earliest Irish, Welsh and Scottish characters in English plays.* Cork: Cork University Press, 1954.
Bliss, Alan. 'A Synge Glossary.' In *Sunshine and the Moon's Delight: A Centenary Tribute to J. M. Synge.* Ed. S. B. Bushrui. Gerrards Cross: Colin Smythe and the American University of Beirut. 1972, pp. 297-316.
Bliss, Alan. *Spoken English in Ireland 1600-1740.* Dublin: Dolmen Press, 1979.
Clark, James M. *The Vocabulary of Anglo-Irish.* 1917; rpt. Folcroft: Folcroft Library Editions, 1974.
Evans, E. Estyn. *Irish Folk Ways.* 1957; rpt. London: Routledge, 1988.
Greene, David. *The Irish Language.* Dublin: The Three Candles, 1966.
Hickey, D. J. and J. E. Doherty: *A Dictionary of Irish History since 1800.* Dublin: Gill and Macmillan, 1980.
Joyce, P. W. *English as We Speak it in Ireland.* 1910; rpt., introd. T. P. Dolan. Dublin: Wolfhound, 1979, 1988.
Taniguchi, Jiro. *A Grammatical Analysis of Artistic Representation of Irish English. With a Brief Discussion of Sounds and Spelling.* Tokyo: Shinozaki Shorin, 1972.
Trudgill, Peter and Jean Hannah. *International English.* 1982; 3rd ed. London: Edward Arnold, 1994.
Wall, Richard. *An Anglo-Irish Dialect Glossary for Joyce's Works.* Gerrards Cross: Colin Smythe, 1986.

ADDENDUM

published after the present volume went to press

Wall, Richard. *A Dictionary and Glossary for the Irish Literary Revival.* Gerrards Cross: Colin Smythe, 1995.

INTRODUCTION

Sounds, Symbols and Spellings

For the purpose of the present glossary, Hiberno-English is considered as if it were one homogeneous language. This is of course a simplification; there are several clearly distinguishable dialects within Hiberno-English, just as there are several quite distinct dialects of Irish. Differences in lexis and pronunciation are particularly noticeable between the English spoken in the northern parts of Ireland and that spoken in the south.

The glossary does not register such variants, and headwords are as a rule not transcribed phonetically. In words of Irish origin it has been found practical in most cases to indicate only an acceptable pronunciation of the Irish original in headword definitions, and to let the degree of 'Irishness' aimed at by the speaker determine the degree of approximation to that original. Other headwords will generally be recognisable from Standard English and require no pronunciation indicator – though allowances must be made for variations in the actual realisation of the individual sounds, which may be considerable without making the word in question unidentifiable to the listener.

As a general rule, Irish words are cited in the spelling and pronunciation used in the 'neutral' or 'core' dialect devised for the English-Irish, Irish-English Pocket Dictionary, *Foclóir Póca*, published by The Department of Education in Dublin.

SYMBOLS

Transcription of Irish words

Irish has two kinds of consonants: one, the 'velarised' or 'broad' variant, sounds rather as if it were followed by [w]; the other, 'slender' or 'palatalised' variant, sounds rather as if it had a following [j]. These distinctions are important for the meanings of the words, i.e. they are phonemic (as they are in e.g. Russian and Polish, but not in English or Welsh or Latin). In the present glossary, Irish sounds are transcribed according to the broad transcription used in the *Foclóir Póca*; this means that velarised consonants are unmarked, while palatalised consonants are indicated by '. In principle, the system thus has a double set of consonants: /b/b'/, /k/k'/, /n/n'/, etc.

Consonant symbols will be familiar from English orthography, with the following exceptions: /x/x'/, representing the unvoiced fricatives as in German *ach*/*ich*, and /ɣ/ɣ'/ representing the corresponding voiced sounds.

Vowel symbols are those of the *Foclóir Póca*, where they are listed as follows:

Vowels	Nearest English Equivalent	Dipthongs	Nearest English Equivalent
/i/	s*i*t	/ai/	*I*
/i:/	m*e*	/au/	c*ow*
/e/	s*e*t	/iə/	p*ia*nist
/e:/	s*ay*	/uə/	fl*ue*nt
/a/	b*a*t		
/a:/	f*ar*		
/o/	s*o*n		
/o:/	m*o*re		
/u/	b*oo*k		
/u:/	wh*o*		
/ə/	*a*bout		

Subject to regional differences, primary stress in Irish usually falls on the first syllable of a word. A major exception occurs in words where the second syllable is long, in which case that syllable may receive primary stress. The glossary only registers stress in Irish words – by placing | before the stressed syllable – if it does not follow these two general rules.

Transcription of English and anglicised words

The symbols used for English and anglicised transcription are the same as those used for Irish words (see above), with the addition of:

þ as in *th*ink
ð as in *th*en   (not in Irish)

/ʌ/ as in d*u*ll
/ɔ/ as in d*o*ll   (not distinctive in Irish)

/ɔ:/ as in *a*ll

/ou/ as in *o*ld

/æə/ as in *ai*r

/ei/ as in m*a*ke

/ʃ/ as in *sh*all   (corresponding to /s'/ in Irish transcription)
/j/ as in *y*es   (corresponding to /ɣ'/ in Irish transcription)

Where it has been found desirable to designate stress in English/anglicised pronunciation, this is symbolised by | as for Irish words.

As signalled by the use of slashes rather than square brackets, transcription of both Irish and English/anglicised words is phonemic, i.e. it represents distinctive units and not actual speech sounds.

ENGLISH WORDS IN HIBERNO-ENGLISH

For historical as well as phonetic and phonological reasons, English is often spoken in Ireland with a distinct accent, the *brogue*. The word is allegedly derived from Irish *bróg* /bro:g/, originally meaning a boot or shoe of untanned hide. It is sometimes used in a wider sense not only of the speech accent, but to include also the syntax and vocabulary of Hiberno-English.

Ireland's geographical isolation in the past meant that the English spoken there was not automatically influenced by the sound changes that affected the English spoken in England, e.g. the great vowel shift of Early Modern English. Moreover, until well into the 19th century, a large majority of the population in Ireland spoke English only as their second language, if at all. They would often have learnt it from Irish-speaking neighbours and teachers, who had themselves acquired it imperfectly, and who rarely handed on an 'English' pronunciation. The result may be described as a compromise between the Irish and English sound registers.

'Phonetic' spellings

The characteristically Hiberno-English pronunciation of English words is rarely reflected in writing nowadays. This may be partly because any deviation from a received pronunciation easily becomes comic, as indeed the brogue was, and still is, a prominent feature of anti-Irish jokes. It may of course also be because non-Standard pronunciations are no longer so marked. Many characteristic phonological features that may be deduced from earlier writings are rarely heard nowadays. This applies i.a. to /fw/ for /hw/, as in the spelling *phwat* for 'what'. Other examples are the use of /ʃ/ for /s/, which appears from spellings like *misht* for 'mist', and a much-quoted line spoken by Shakespeare's only Irish character, Captain Macmorris in *Henry V*: *What ish my nation?*

In Hiberno-English the front vowel closest to that of English 'get' is higher than in Received Pronunciation (a raising of /e/ to /i/ that took place chiefly before nasals). Hence spellings like *rint* for 'rent' and *gintleman* for 'gentleman', as in the facetious reference to the pig as the 'gintleman who pays the rint'. Again, the diphthong /ai/ of 'I', 'Irish' often has a more rounded first element in Ireland than in Received Pronunciation, giving spellings like *Oi, Oirish*. The diphthong /ou/, on the other hand, may have a less rounded and more open first element, as reflected in the spellings *ould* and *auld* for 'old'.

Until well into this century 'phonetic' spellings like this were common, especially in writings that made it their errand to emphasize the difference of all things Irish. In such attempts to lend an 'Irish' flavour to an English text, 'tea' regularly appears as *tay*, for instance, reflecting Modern English orthography's attempt to represent an earlier /e:/, which was retained in Ireland but became /i:/ in Received Pronunciation. The pronunciation is aptly reflected in the spelling of 'easy' in the phrase *a Paddy-go-aisy type*, which at the same time captures the Irishman's reputation of being easy-going to a fault along with a generic name for any Irishman (*Paddy*, from Ireland's patron saint, *Patrick*).

The Irish substratum under much Hiberno-English pronunciation is also apparent in the remarkable conventional spellings of English /þ/ð/ and Irish /t/d/. A simplified explanation not venturing beyond the broad transcription used in this book might run as follows:

There are no dental fricatives in Irish, so, instead of /þ/ð/, Irish people speaking English would use the closest counterparts they were familiar with: non-palatal dental stops. English scribes, expecting to hearing a dental fricative /þ/ð/ and hearing what was really a dental stop, Irish /t/d/, registered this as a stop, and vice versa: when they expected to hear a stop and heard what to them sounded like a fricative (but was really a dental stop), they wrote *th* or *dh*. The *t* for 'th' in *tird* and the *th* for 't' in *Pether* thus denote basically the same sound, viz. the non-palatal dental stop.

The spellings *th* and *dh* for Standard English 't' and 'd' occur notably before a following /r/ or /ər/, where English /t/d/ are replaced by Irish /t/d/. These spellings were almost mandatory in popular 19th century writing purporting to reflect the actual pronunciation of Irish characters. In our own century, the Dublin plays of Seán O'Casey offer numerous examples: *murdher, betther, thrying, Fluther,* et al.

Again, *dis* and *dat* were common 'phonetic' spellings for 'this' and 'that', and *de* for 'the'; perhaps the fact that these words are commonly unstressed encouraged a less deliberate pronunciation. In James Joyce's *Ulysses*, the sound thus transcribed – a stop instead of a fricative – is ridiculed by Mr. Dedalus bemoaning his shiftless family: *'O weeping God, the things I married into. De boys up in de hayloft.'* The pronunciation – Irish /d/t/ for English /ð/þ/, registered in English script as *d/t* – was by no means confined to the uneducated classes. Tradition has it that /d/ (i.e. Irish /d/) was used for the /ð/ of Received Pronunciation in these cases by no less august a personage than President de Valera, and also by Lady Gregory, one of the renowned founders and playwrights of the Abbey Theatre.

The differences between spoken English in Ireland and Received Pronunciation such as those mentioned above are generally not distinctive. There is an outstanding example, however, in James Joyce's punning use of *wake/weak* in the title *Finnegans Wake*, which may mean either 'The all-night watch ('wake') over Finnegan's corpse', or 'Finnegan is weak (i.e. drunk)'; the reference is to a song about the hilarious wake of an Irish labourer, Tim Finnegan.

IRISH WORDS IN HIBERNO-ENGLISH

Since the English and Irish sound registers are different in many respects, spelling an Irish word was no easy job for a scribe working with the 26 letters of the English alphabet. This goes some way towards explaining the many alternative spellings that occur in all but the most recent texts. Irish elbow pipes, for instance, may be rendered i.a. *uilleann, villein,* or *woollen* pipes, reflecting perhaps partly the fact that the initial vowel was not familiar to the scribe, partly dialect variation in the actual pronunciation of the Irish word for elbow (*uillinn*).

INTRODUCTION

Another approximate notation concerns the Hiberno-English pronunciation of the Irish vowel in a word like *bán* (fair-haired), which is usually somewhat more rounded than the English /a:/, and is often written *aw* in an English context – which again may encourage a pronunciation closer to the English *born* than *barn*. The Irish *cailín bán* (fair-haired young girl) thus appears in English spelling as the *Colleen Bawn*. The title of a well-known drinking song, the *Cruskeen Lawn*, has undergone similar treatment (from Irish *crúiscín*, little jug + *lán*, full). The anglicised spelling of the name *Seán* as *Shawn* is also a case in point.

Colleen and *Cruskeen* merit a further word of explanation, along with the many other words that end in *-een*, the Irish diminutive *ín* /i:n'/. In Irish these endings are preceded by a palatalised consonant, and the final consonant is likewise palatalised; but the palatalisation is not transferred to the anglicised form of the word, since palatalised consonants have no phonemic importance in English. On the lips of English speakers, *cailín* /cal'i:n'/ becomes /kɔli:n/, and *crúiscín* /kru:s'k'i:n'/ is usually pronounced /kruski:n/; in both cases, stress may vary according to i.a. sentence stress.

The symbol ´ in Irish orthography designates length. It is not always used when Irish words are transposed, otherwise unchanged, into an English context; an example is the name of one of Ireland's two houses of parliament, the Dáil, which commonly appears as the 'Dail'.

MUTATION IN IRISH WORDS

Before attempting to look up a word in an Irish dictionary, it is useful to have a rudimentary knowledge of the way many initial consonants may be changed according to a complicated system of mutation that all living Celtic languages have in common. Broadly speaking, the pronunciation of a given sound might originally be modified – 'mutated' – by the character of the preceding sound. When the preceding sound disappeared, as many sounds did over the centuries, the mutation became a matter of grammar, affecting not only isolated words but also words associated in groups, such as certain juxtapositions of article, noun and adjective.

For example, the definite article in the nominative singular is *an* /ə(n)/ in the masculine and feminine alike. Yet in a sense it is not the same *an*, because it changes the first consonant of the following noun if that noun is feminine, but not if it is masculine. 'Boy' in Irish is *buachaill* /buəxəl'/ and 'the boy' is *an buachaill*. 'Woman' is *bean* /b'an/, but because of mutation 'the woman' is *an bhean* /ə(n) v'an/. The mutation of *b* to *bh*, pronounced /v/, is also operative in the *Shan Van Vocht* (anglicised spelling), the Poor Old Woman who symbolises Ireland: in Irish dictionaries, Shan will be found under *sean* (old), Van under *bean* (woman, mutated as *bhean*), and Vocht under *bocht* (poor, mutated as *bhocht*); the changes of *b* to *bh* here are determined by the position and gender of noun and adjective.

This mutation may be either *aspiration*, which turns certain consonants into fricatives, or *eclipsis*, which makes voiceless consonants voiced and voiced consonants nasal. The present glossary offers several instances, especially among phrases of address and endearment, the mutation regularly coming into play after the vocative particle *a* and the possessive *mo*. Among well-known examples are *mavourneen*, 'my dear', where the medial *v* represents a mutated *m* (*muirnín*

/muːrnˈiːnʲ/ = sweetheart); and *machree,* 'my dear', the *ch* /x/ signifying the mutated form of *c* /k/ (*croí* /kriː/ = heart).

In Modern Irish, mutation affects consonants basically as follows:

Aspiration

/p/pʼ/ become /f/fʼ/, written *ph* as in *Oifig an Phoist* (Post Office)
/t/tʼ/ become /h/, written *th* as in *do Thadhg* (to Tadhg)
/k/kʼ/ become /x/xʼ/, written *ch* as in *A Chara* (Dear ... [in letters])
/f/fʼ/ become silent, written *fh* as in *Ard Fheis* ('High Festival')
/s/sʼ= ʃ/ become /h/xʼ/, written *sh* as in *ó Sheán* (from Seán)
/b/bʼ/ become /v/vʼ/, written *bh* as in *mo bhean* (my wife)
/d/dʼ/ become /ɣ/ɣʼ=j/, written *dh* as in *ar dheis* (to the right)
/g/gʼ/ become /ɣ/ɣʼ=j/, written *gh* as in *don gharsún* (to the boy)
/m/mʼ/ become /v/vʼ/, written *mh* as in *mo mhuirnín* (my dear)

As appears from the above list, aspiration is indicated by adding *h*: *ch*, *mh*, etc. In the traditional Irish script that was in use up to the middle of this century, the change was indicated by placing a dot above the letter in question: ċ, ṁ, etc.

Eclipsis

/p/pʼ become /b/bʼ/, written *bp* as in *i bpáirc* (in a field)
/t/tʼ/ become /d/dʼ/, written *dt* as in *ag an dtigh* (at the house)
/k/kʼ/ become /g/gʼ/, written *gc* as in *seacht gcapaill* (seven horses)
/f/fʼ/ become /v/vʼ/, written *bhf* as in *leis an bhfear* (with the man)
/b/bʼ/ become /m/mʼ/, written *mb* as in *i mbád* (in the boat)
/d/dʼ/ become /n/nʼ/, written *nd* as in *i nDoire* (in Derry)
/g/gʼ/ become /ŋ/ŋʼ/, written *ng* as in *i ngrá* (in love)

THE TWO LANGUAGES IN IRELAND

The Irish language was established in Ireland by some of the Celtic peoples who overran Europe a few centuries before the birth of Christ. It belongs to the Celtic branch of Indo-European languages, and is related to the languages of Wales, Cornwall and Brittany, and, more closely, to those of the Scottish Highlands and the Isle of Man. Together with Irish, these last two languages are sometimes termed *Gaelic* (*Irish Gaelic, Scottish* or *Scots Gaelic*, and *Manx Gaelic*). Manx is now extinct, and it has become customary to reserve the name *Gaelic* for Scottish Gaelic, and to call the historical language of Ireland *Irish*. Outside matters of language, *Gaelic* is still used in Ireland with reference to native, non-English culture, as in *Gaelic football*. *Erse* (a term not often used nowadays) is the Scottish Gaelic form of the word *Irish*; it is properly applicable only to Scottish Gaelic.

English has been spoken in parts of Ireland since the Norman invasions of the Middle Ages. Probably not by the invaders themselves, for they spoke Norman French, but by their followers and descendants, who settled in a narrow margin of land on the east coast, establishing themselves most securely in the towns. Thus was laid the foundation of what became known as *the Pale*, the area of English jurisdiction around Dublin and northwards, up to and including Dundalk. The early settlers seem to have succumbed easily to the influence of their adopted country, however, for already in 1366 the *Statutes of Kilkenny* found it necessary to forbid marriage between invaders and natives, and to decree that all Englishmen must speak English, use English surnames and follow English customs. These statutes were largely unsuccessful, and when in the succeeding centuries the Irish vernacular came to be associated with the Catholic faith, its status as the language of the oppressed was consolidated.

The distribution of the two languages was to mirror a sharply polarised society. On one side were the Catholic, Irish-speaking peasants, who knew no English; on the other, the Protestant landowners, who were often English by descent and education, and who knew no Irish. Apart from certain areas in the north of the country, Irish was for centuries the everyday language of a large majority of the population, while English was the prestige language of business, law and politics. Until well into the 19th century, it was mainly the landowners and urban upper classes who used English as a family language. It was of course a distinctive variety of English, differing from the standard language in pronunciation, syntax, and – as evidenced in the present glossary – vocabulary.

The decline of Irish

Several factors contributed to the decline of the native language that made itself felt early in the 19th century. For one thing, when Penal Laws discriminating against Catholics were repealed in the 1790s, thousands of people found that there were undreamt-of opportunities within their reach. They naturally opted for English as the surest way up the social ladder, encouraged in this by the popular and influential political leader Daniel O'Connell. Again, when National Schools giving education free of charge were established in the 1830s, the Irish language was simply excluded from their curriculum.

It was the Great Famine of the 1840s, however, that dealt the most serious blow to the Irish vernacular. In those disastrous years, about one million people died and another million emigrated, and it was among those two million that Irish had been strongest. To the survivors who stayed at home, English seemed the 'key to the golden gate of America', and it was a key that not many parents withheld from their children. With such motivation, it took no more than two generations before Ireland became largely English-speaking.

Scholarly interest in Irish

But while social and economic pressures were killing Irish as a spoken language, other forces were at work preserving what was left. Among the educated classes there was a widespread interest in the old Gaelic literature of Ireland and Scotland. This interest went back to the late 18th century, when a Scottish schoolmaster, James Macpherson, published his so-called translations of old poetry, allegedly collected in the Gaelic-speaking Highlands of Scotland and attributed to a bard named Ossian. It was not ancient poetry that Macpherson had saved from oblivion, however. The poems of Ossian were a strange mixture of his own, a concoction of fragments of genuine old Gaelic stories dealing with the exploits of heroic warriors in a far distant past before the coming of Christianity.

Though his translations were in a sense forgeries, Macpherson did a great service to Gaelic language and literature by drawing attention to it and encouraging scholars to study and publish old manuscripts. In Ireland, his works inspired the first anthology of secular Irish literature: Charlotte Brooke's *Reliques of Irish Poetry* (1789), where the originals were printed in the old Irish script and accompanied by scholarly notes and translations. Interest in Ireland's early literature and antiquities grew throughout the 19th century, and linguistic studies were published by both Irish and Continental scholars. Two of the landmarks in the study of the Irish language were John O'Donovan's *A Grammar of the Irish Language* (1845) and Rudolf Thurneysen's *A Grammar of Old Irish*, which first appeared in German in 1909.

There were many societies for the study of ancient Irish culture. The most influential was the Gaelic League, whose aim was no less than to revive Irish as the national language and to create a modern literature in Irish. It had branches all over the country, with Irish classes where the native language was taught by voluntary travelling teachers.

Hiberno-English as a medium of literature

The Gaelic League was founded in 1893 by Douglas Hyde, a distinguished scholar and collector of Irish folk material who was to become the first President of Ireland. 1893 also saw the publication of one of his best-known books: *Love Songs of Connacht* /kɔnəxt/. This is a collection of oral poetry that Hyde took down from Irish speakers, printing it in the original form as he heard it along with his own verse translation, and also with a literal prose translation – as he had presented English translations along with Irish originals in a prose collection of folk-tales published a few years earlier. Hyde's English was equally removed from the artificial language of the Stage Irishman (see Appendix) and the stilted literary style commonly found in most other collections of folk-lore. Popular as they were, however, his books in a way defeated their own purpose of championing the Irish language, because Hyde's translations – especially the literal prose translations of the *Love Songs* – showed how well the English spoken in Ireland lent itself to literature. In doing so, his work helped to trigger off an influential literary movement that grew up around the turn of the century, led by writers like W. B. Yeats, who believed that it was possible to create in the English language a literature that was independent of English ideals, and rooted in the character and history of the Irish people.

This movement, originating in a dislike of the English commercial theatre, became known as *The Irish Literary Revival* or *Renaissance*. It drew its inspiration from rural Irish culture and traditions, and was liberal in its use of linguistic features taken from what was then often dimissed as a mere non-Standard dialect. Characteristic examples from the work of the dramatist J. M. Synge include many of the words listed in the present glossary, and syntactical features like the use of *after* + verbal noun to express the immediate past (*'The people are after passing to the fair of Clash'*;*'Amn't I after seeing the love-light of the star of knowledge shining from her brow?'*); the omission of the relative pronoun as subject (*'A hat [that] is suited for a wedding day'*; *'Where is the bit of new rope, Cathleen, [that] was bought in Connemara?'*); and absolute constructions with *and*, where Standard English would use a dependent clause (*'There was a star up against the moon, and it rising in the night'*; *'What way will I live and the girls with me, and I an old woman looking for the grave?'*). The Revival dramatists offer numerous examples, too, of the non-Standard use of *do* with *to be*, as in *'Those mountainy men do be poor'* (Lady Gregory), and *'I do be thinking sometimes ... we might be put in the way of making Patrick a priest'* (W. B. Yeats); this usage was captured in the title of an early satire on 'peasant plays' that has since become a catch-phrase: *The Mist That Does Be On The Bog*.

Kiltartan is the name given to an extreme form of Hiberno-English heavily dependent on non-Standard structures like those quoted above. It was Lady Gregory who first gave rise to the use of the word *Kiltartan* in a non-geographic sense; it is the name of a district near her home, Coole Park in County Galway, which she had used in some of the titles of her books of folk-tales and folk history. A particular feature is the 'Kiltartan infinitive', as in these examples from her plays: *'There must be a great deal of spending in a hundred pounds. It's a pity some honest man not to be the better of that'; 'He that was used to the mountain to be closed up inside of that [gaol]!'*

Northern Hiberno-English

The linguistic situation was different in the northern parts of Ireland, which had received a large influx of English-speaking colonists in the so-called plantations of the early 17th century, and where the English language has been dominant ever since. It was not the same English that had been introduced into the southern part of the country (which may broadly be called the English of England), but that spoken in the north of England and especially in the south-west of Scotland, where many of the settlers came from. The constant to-ing and fro-ing that went on for centuries between Scotland and the north-eastern corner of Ireland is still evident in both accent and vocabulary: *sheugh* (ditch), *clarty* (dirty), and a host of other words are common to the northern variants of Hiberno-English and the regional dialects of northern England and Lowland Scots.

But the Celtic substratum is unmistakably there, too – in place names, for example. Two roads in Belfast which may be said to represent the extremes of the conflict in Northern Ireland have in fact names going back to a common Celtic past: *Shankill Road*, a stronghold of Ulster Protestant Loyalism, is originally *Bóthar na Seanchille* /boːhər nə sˈanxˈilˈə/, 'the road of the old church'. Its opposite pole, the road associated perhaps more than any other with Nationalism and Catholicism – *Falls Road* – also has a name of Irish origin: *Bóthar na bhFál* /boːhər nə vaːl/, meaning 'the road of the hedges'.

Irish to-day

Irish is an official language of the Irish State, where it is universally accepted as a badge of national identity. It is a compulsory subject in all grant-aided schools, and a working knowledge of the language is required for appointments in the Civil Service and other professions. An Irish language radio station has been broadcasting since 1972. There are usually several daily programmes in Irish on the main television station, and in 1995 an all-Irish television station is due to be launched.

Though various other provisions have been made for encouraging the use of Irish, English is by far the dominant language in Ireland. The rough figure given for Irish-speakers to-day is 100.000, but this covers many degrees of competence, and it is estimated that there have been no more than 30.000 habitual native speakers at any one time within the past half century.

Irish-speaking areas are called *Gaeltachts* /geːltəxts/ and are found chiefly on the western seaboard of Ireland: in Donegal, Galway and on the Dingle peninsula, with an inland pocket around Macroom in County Cork, and a smaller pocket in County Meath. The Irish spoken in these areas is clearly distinguishable as different dialects, none of which corresponds in all features to the 'core' dialect devised for the Department of Education's Irish-English dictionary, which is used in the present glossary.

GLOSSARY

It is beyond the scope of this work to register or exemplify all alternative spellings, and it has been found practical to register as headwords only those variants whose initial syllable may make identification difficult: Cile –>Sheela, badhach –>bodach, dilisk –>dulse, gassan –>gossoon, etc. Variant spellings in following syllables (often unstressed) may occur in quotations, but are not listed as headwords: chiseller (= chiselur), eskar (= esker), etc.; this also applies to the numerous instances of *th/dh* for Standard English 't'/'d', and vice versa (see Introduction).

Headwords of Irish origin may be pronounced with varying degrees of approximation to the original, which is given in the 'core' pronunciation used in the *Foclóir Póca* (see Introduction). In a few cases, a generally acceptable anglicised pronunciation has been suggested.

Examples are cited in chronological order according to authors' dates of birth. Surnames alone are given where this is sufficient for identification (see list of Authors Quoted for full names and dates).

absentee Landlord not living on his estate; the prototype of exploiting and uncaring landowners.

The Absentee (Title, Edgeworth).

I starved to feed the absentee with rent (R. Murphy).

No-one would dare to venture so far out [on the lake] for fear of the bailiffs who still ruled the water for an absentee landlord (Devlin).

a'cushla Term of endearment (from Irish voc. of *cuisle* /kus'l'ə/ = pulse).

'Come here to me, acushla!' says I to him (Somerville and Ross).

Two ladies of Galway, called Catherine and Anna, / Whom some call Acushla and some call –>Alanna (Shaw).

a'gra	Term of endearment (from Irish voc. of *grá* /gra:/ = love). See also –>grah.

O Woman of Three Cows, agra! don't let your tongue thus rattle! (Mangan trans.). |
| aim's ace | A very small distance (properly 'ambs ace' = double ace, the lowest throw in dice; from OFr.).

'[He] made a woeful wipe at him one time with his –>caman and I declare to God he was within an aim's ace of getting it at the side of his temple' (Joyce). |
| aisling | Vision poem (from Irish *aisling* /as'l'əŋ/ = vision); in the 18th century typically bound up with the Stuart cause: a poet, wandering in a meadow, meets a lovely maiden (Ireland) mourning for her exiled love (a Stuart prince).

He had his aislings and laments for the Catholic –>big houses (Flanagan).

In his nasal voice he intoned the –>Ulster aislings (Montague).

Aisling (Title, Heaney). |
| a'lanna | Term of endearment (from Irish voc. of *leanbh* /l'anəv/ = child).

'Come along, allana, an make paste for the pie' (Shaw).

She almost stopped calling Eily by her pet name, which was Alannah (E. O'Brien). |
| alley | See –>ball alley. |
| alpeen | Knobbed stick (from Irish *ailp* /al'p'/ = knob + dimin.).

A countryman with an alpeen (Thackeray). |
| amadán | See –>omadaun. |

American wake	Party held on the eve of an emigration. See –>wake.

'Like an American wake, when someone is going away' (Behan).

We got closer than ever / until it came his turn to leave / after the American wake (Egan). |
| **amhrán** | Song (from Irish *amhrán* /aura:n/). *Amhran na bhFiann* /aura:n nə v'iən/ = The –>'Soldiers' Song', Ireland's National Anthem.

One councillor had complained that when a local person tried to make a complaint to a group of police officers the officers started singing <u>Amhrán na bhFiann</u> back to him (Irish Times). |
| **Anglo-Irish** | The following uses may conveniently be distinguished:

1. Of England and Ireland.

The Anglo-Irish summit on December 3rd (Irish Times).

2. Of literature written in English by Irish or Irish-based writers.

IASAIL = The International Association for the Study of Anglo-Irish Literature.

3. Of the English language spoken in Ireland, = Hiberno-English.

The Vocabulary of Anglo-Irish (see Select Bibliography).

4. Of the Anglican –> Ascendancy class.

By a number of Anglo-Irish landlords this abrogation of their power ... was felt as a bitter blow (Bowen).

'He was an Anglo-Irishman.' 'In the name of God, what's that?' 'A Protestant with a horse' (Behan). |
| **Anglo-Irish War** | See –>War of Independence. |

An Óige	The Irish Youth Hostel Association (from Irish def. art. *an* /ən/ + *óige* /o:g'ə/ = youth).

An Óige have planned a New Year's Day Walk in the Wicklow Mountains (Irish Times). |
| **An Post** | The Irish Postal Service (from Irish def. art. *an* /ə(n)/ + *post* /post/).

An Post has identified the main problems causing delays in the delivery of letters in the Dublin area (Irish Times). |
| **An Taisce** | Ireland's conservation body (from Irish def. art. *an* /ə(n)/ + *taisce* /tas'k'ə/ = store, treasure).

Tailor's Hall in Back Lane, built between 1704 and 1706 and lovingly restored by An Taisce (Irish Times). |
| **¹Áras an ¹Uachtaráin** | The residence of the President of Ireland in Phoenix Park, Dublin (from Irish *áras* /a:rəs/ = house + gen. of *an uachtarán* /ən uəxtəra:n/ = the president).

Gathering darkness over Aras an Uachtaráin, the old Vice-Regal lodge (Montague).

Outside the gates we used to lie in the grass / Making love outside Áras an Uachtaráin (Durcan).

The abortion issue was invoked by –>Fianna Fail in the most naked way with –>TD John Browne's remarks about the prospect of abortion referral clinics in Áras an Uachtaráin (Irish Times). |
| **ard chomhairle** | 'High Council' (from Irish *ard* /a:rd/ = high + mutated form (/xo:rl'ə/) of *comhairle* /ko:rl'ə/ = council).

The –>Sinn Fein ard-chomhairle member, Mr Martin McGuinness (Irish Times). |
| **ard fheis** | General (annual) meeting (from Irish *ard* /a:rd/ = high + mutated form (/es'/) of *feis* /f'es'/ = festival. See –>feish. |

His tenure will be remembered chiefly for his 'satirical' comedy delivered ... at the 1991 ard fheis (Irish Times).

In purely political terms, he will be the Brian Lenihan of many a →Fianna Fail ard fheis who brought the grassroots to an orgasmic peak by the time Charles J. Haughey bounded onto the stage (Irish Times).

ard-rí 'High King', an ancient Irish title (from Irish *ard* /a:rd/ = high + *rí* /ri:/ = king).

[They] can recognize him [i.e. Parnell] as their uncrowned king, a Protestant <u>ard-rí</u> of a largely Catholic people (Montague).

a¹roon Term of endearment (from Irish voc. of *rún* /ru:n/ = secret, secret treasure).

Eileen Aroon (Title, song).

Come back, aroon, to the land of thy birth (Song).

¹arrah Interjection.

'Arrah, shut yer mouth!" says the bandmasther (Somerville and Ross).

'Arra would you mind what the like of him would tell you?' (Shaw).

Ascendancy The Anglican landowning and professional classes that formerly constituted a social elite.

Easter 1916 began to sweep away the Ascendancy (Lewis).

They invent a romantic Irish tradition which just ignores the English ascendancy (Murdoch).

ashplant Stick made of ashwood, often from an ash sapling.

Like a drover with an ashplant (Heaney).

Most of the other men were unknown and identified by their big boots ... and their ash plants (E. O'Brien).

a'shtor Term of endearment (from Irish voc. of *stór* /sto:r/ = wealth).

'Can you do it for me, asthore?' he asked the horse (K. O'Brien).

'Eamon, a stór, we're going to lose him' (Tóibín).

auld See –>ould.

Auxiliaries Mainly demobilised British Army officers, recruited in 1920 to augment the –>RIC; also 'Auxies'. The Auxiliaries were notorious for brutality, as were the –>Black and Tans.

'For God's sake tell her to go to hell out of this — she's worse than the Auxsie' (O'Casey).

On the night of 11 December Cork was sacked by Auxiliaries and –>Black and Tans after a patrol had been ambushed (Farrell).

avenue Approach to a house through a park or garden; the equivalent of a 'drive' in England.

I doubt whether the avenue at Chatsworth is fifty miles long, as was the Martins' at Ballynahinch (Robinson).

Its long rhododendron drive — or avenue, as they say in Ireland (Trevor).

a'vic Familiar mode of address to a young man (from Irish voc. of *mac* /mak/ = son, boy).

'I believe you're right, avic; and — ' 'Vic me no longer, father' (Carleton).

'Come on, a Mhic [/ə vik/], straighten up for Christ's sake – or at least for Ireland's sake' (Durcan).

bacach	Lame man, tramp (from Irish *bacach* /bakəx/).

'As I was going down the bohereen [–>boreen], I met an old <u>bocaugh,</u> that ... used always to sleep in our barn, while he staid in the neighbourhood' (Croker).

He burned the bacach's little house / On last St. Brigid's Night (Campbell). |
| **badhach** | See –>bodach. |
| **bainin** | See –>bawneen. |
| **ball alley** | Alley where –>handball is played.

I looked out for the house licensed to sell beer and tobacco ... Above it was the great wall of the ball alley, denounced by Father James Browne in his sermons (G. Moore).

The tall echoing concrete of the ball alley (Montague). |
| **ball of malt** | Glass of whiskey.

My father likes to have a ball of malt in the bar (Higgins).

'After a day of listening to rubbish it's a pleasure to take a ball of malt with him.' Frances giggled. When my father called a glass of whiskey a ball of malt Frances always giggled (Trevor).

Silas strode to the deserted bar and rapped upon it with his knuckles ... 'A ball of malt, my man' (Banville). |
| **Ballyhooley** | Trouble, fuss (from the name of a village near Fermoy in County Cork, formerly notorious for its –>faction fights).

A journey, that would be sure to entail 'Ballyhooley' upon his devoted head when he got home, for being away so long (Kickham). |
| **Banba** | /banva/ Poetic name for Ireland (from *Banbha*, a queen of the –>Tuatha Dé –>Danaan). |

And I will kneel at the Latin stone / That covers the Virgin Tree, / And pray that I may look on the dawn / That breaks on Banba free! (Campbell).

'Oul' [–>ould] Mulligan would call himself a descendant of the true –>Gaels of Banba' (O'Casey).

banbh See –>bonnav.

banjaxed Defeated, overwhelmed (a humorous term, perhaps formed by association with 'banged', 'bashed', 'smashed').

'A man that is nearly banjaxed from the principle of the Atomic Theory' (F. O'Brien).

Jimmy had finally had to have an operation on his bowel; otherwise, as he confided sheepishly ... he'd be properly banjacksed for the rest of his days (Brady).

¹**banshee** A spirit said to wail outside the windows of a house when someone is about to die (from Irish *bean sí* /b'an s'i:/ = woman of the fairies). See –>shee.

'The very Banshee that my grandfather heard under Sir Patrick's window a few days before his death' (Edgeworth).

Sitting on a heap of –>turf by the kitchen fire, [she] drew her shawl closer about her shoulders, and thought gruesomely of the Banshee (Somerville and Ross).

The ice-cream man rumbled down the street blowing his banshee horn (Brown).

bap Soft roll or bun, often diamond-shaped (etym. unknown).

Baking bread for guerillas, Leila sees herself as a revolutionary Jesus blessing the fishes and feeding the multitude: and how now about a bomb in the Belfast bap or the –>barmbrack (Kiely).

Some of the [harvest] men lie down immediately ... and I see again the white flesh above the rolled-up sleeves of their shirts as they reach for the cheese and sandwiches and baps (Devlin).

barmbrack Traditional Halloween cake or loaf with raisins, often containing a lucky trinket (from Irish *bairín* /bar'i:n'/ = loaf + *breac* /b'r'ak/= speckled).

Maria superintended the distribution of the barmbrack and saw that every woman got her four slices (Joyce).

Every girl's parcel contained a barmbrack and apples (E. O'Brien).

barony Division of a county. See also –>townland.

Our way lay through the highly cultivated baronies of Forth and Bargy (Hall).

Across the ridge of the barony a fan of light from a lighthouse swung its arc on shore and sea and sky (MacMahon).

barracks Formerly a residence for soldiers. Nowadays usually a rural police station, with residential quarters.

'Across the Green, there is the police-barracks, we never called it the police station, with barbed wire now and sandbags and reinforced concrete' (Kiely).

'There is nobody left in the district worth blowing up ... it can only have been the Civic Guard [–>Garda] barracks' (Behan).

The Barracks (Title, McGahern).

bawn[1] Grassland; often the green field where cows are brought to be milked, or simply the farmyard. Also used of other, ancient enclosures (from Irish *bán* /ba:n/ = grassland).

He sauntered over to the bawne of Ballintober, and climbed ... to the top of one of the towers of that beautiful ruin (W. Wilde).

'He has –>lepped off the stile. He is coming up the bawn' (Fitzmaurice).

The house ... flashed across the chestnut-marshalled lawn / a few lit windows on a bullock bawn (Hartnett).

bawn²   White, fair-haired (from Irish *bán* /ba:n/ = white, fair). See also –>white-haired, –>white-headed.

'God bless you, boy bawn' (J. B. Keane).

bawneen   A loose whitish jacket of home-made undyed flannel (from Irish *báinín* /ba:n'i:n'/, from *bán* /ba:n/ = white + dimin.).

'He seems an Aran fisher, for he wears / The flannel bawneen and the cow-hide shoe' (Yeats).

He was wearing the same bainin coat that Mico knew him in seven years ago (Macken).

The clothing that the country people around Galway had long ago ... Nice white báinín, frieze breeches and a wide hat like a Spaniard's (Iremonger trans.).

Be'dad   = 'By Dad', 'By God'.

'Bedad if they weren't the most intelligent hounds in Ireland it's dead long ago they'd be of hunger' (G. Moore).

I thought that hunger would soon make an end of me at school, but bedad it wasn't so (Flower trans.).

beehive hut   Hut shaped like a beehive, built by early hermits. See –>clochaun.

Where the old monks ... flocked in thousands, putting off humanity and building themselves little beehive huts and Eskimo oratories fitter for seagulls than men (O'Connor).

And so I had come to this penitential isle (there are beehive huts in the hills) (Banville).

Be'gob   = 'By God'.

'Begob, there's Father Hannigan; I must be off' (Kickham).

Be′gor = 'By God'.

'Begor! you proved very good, miss!' (Somerville and Ross).

Be′gorra = 'By God'.

Have ye got the parcel there for Mrs. White? / Ye haven't! Oh, begorra! / Say it's comin' down tomorra (French).

[The servants] were wild and garrulous, speaking a strange language in which she was disappointed at never hearing the word 'Begorrah' (M. Keane).

Beltaine The month of May (from Irish *Bealtaine* /bˈaltənə/ = May 1st, when there was a pagan festival in honour of the god *Bél*).

Beltaine (Title, Yeats ed.).

biddable Docile, ready to do what is bidden.

'They were fine grandchildren, fine biddable boys' (McLaverty).

He liked his women biddable (White).

The wilful, unbiddable girl in a Victorian romance (Kiely).

biddy Old woman (from the proper name Bridget).

In a curtainless cubicle a fat old biddy sat on the side of the bed fumbling with her suspenders (Banville).

Big House A landowner's residence.

The workmen that came up from the village to the Big House spoke it [i.e. Irish] always (G. Moore).

The heyday of this –>Anglo-Irish enclave was the eighteenth century ... all about the country they built gracious houses (each to be known to the native tenantry as 'The Big House') (S. O'Faolain).

She had taken care to dress suitably for her visit to the big house (J. Johnston).

black   Black-hearted, sinister; strange, unknown (cf. Irish *dubh gall* /duv gal/ = black foreigner, said of Scandinavian invaders). See also –>hag.

They were 'Black Protestants', all of them, in virtue of their descent from a godly soldier of Cromwell (Somerville and Ross).

'I'm a black stranger. You never seen me before' (Molloy).

Black and Tans   Recruits enlisted in 1920 as a reinforcement for the –>RIC; notorious for their brutal regime. They were nicknamed Black and Tans after a famous pack of foxhounds, owing to their uniforms of khaki worn with the black-green caps and belts of the police. Often called merely 'Tans'. See also –>Auxiliaries.

Gypsy broke the silence to say that a lorryload of Tans had gone past two hours ago (S. O'Faolain).

Any of the houses that entertained the Black and Tans, had officers for dinners and parties, they'd be on the list (Tóibín).

blackthorn   Stout cudgel or walking stick made of the stem of the sloe, a common thorny bush.

Every body with a broad Irish grin on his face, and everybody with his blackthorn (G. Moore).

Mr. Prendergast took his blackthorn stick from the hall stand and went outside (J. Johnston).

blanket bog   Comparatively shallow –>bog that 'blankets' steep slopes.

GLOSSARY

When he stripped off the blanket bog / The soft-piled centuries / Fell open like a –>glib (Heaney).

blarney Smooth, persuasive talk (from Blarney Castle near Cork; the person who kisses a certain stone there is endowed with the gift of blarney). Also verb.

'I don't want to be petted and blarneyed' (Shaw).

They were formidable people those adults ... Not at all like the image of them propagated abroad, as being full of bluff and yarn and blarney (E. O'Brien).

blather Voluble nonsense. Also verb.

I prefer the elusive / rhapsody of blackbirds / to the garrulous blather / of men and women (Heaney).

Let the social workers and the do-gooders blather on about –>'itinerants' or –>'travellers', the –>Gardai held the fort against –>tinkers (Brady).

bocaugh See –>bacach.

bodagh Lout (from Irish *bodach* /bodəx/). Also 'badhach'.

'He's none of your proud, stingy, upsthart <u>bodaghs</u> — none of your beggarly –>half-sirs' (Carleton).

'Swindled them all, skivvies and badhachs from the county Meath, ay, his own kidney too' (Joyce).

bodhran Drum made by stretching the dried skin of a goat or dog across a ring of ash (from Irish *bodhrán* /baura:n/).

Davy Dunn, the bodhrawn-maker, was visited by a distinguished lawyer and an eminent judge from San Francisco. They purchased two bodhrawns (J. B. Keane).

The –>piper, a cadaverous fellow with a shock of lank black hair hanging over one eye, struck up another tune, the bodhran joined in with its truculent booming (Banville).

bog

Marshy ground, which covers a considerable part of the surface of Ireland (from Irish *bog* /bog/ = bog, soft part). See also –>blanket bog.

'And what's all that black swamp out yonder, Sir Kit?' says she. 'My bog, me dear,' says he (Edgeworth).

[He] looked out of the window at what he knew to be a bog. He did not make the mistake of thinking it a moor, as some Englishmen might (Longford).

bog-hole

Wet trench left after cutting peat. See preceding entry.

'He fell into a bog-hole one night after taking a few drinks too many' (Lavin).

The bogholes might be Atlantic seepage / The wet centre is bottomless (Heaney).

bogtrotter

Derogatory term for an Irishman, esp. implying a peasant background. See –>bog.

Sneering at the young bog-trotter's pretensions to his fair daughter's hand (Farrell).

Somewhere in his heart every one of us is a bogtrotter (Heaney).

Her classmates pursued her around the playground, mimicking her accent and calling her a 'bog-trotter' (Irish Times).

bold

Often said of children, = naughty, forward (cf. Irish *dána*, which means both 'bold' and 'forward').

[The Irish nursemaids] would rebuke my naughtiness with a mild 'Ah, don't be so bold, Master Cecil!' (Lewis).

Our figures of authority dislike this ... response and interpret it as recalcitrance or defiance, both of which are labelled 'boldness'. Being labelled 'a bold girl' is fierce criticism (Devlin).

bollav

Dumb, stupid fellow (from Irish *balbh* /baləv/ = dumb).

'Tell me not to tamper with the mind of this bollav' (J. B. Keane).

bolly   See –>booley.

bona fide   Person living at a distance of more than three miles and therefore regarded as a traveller, who was formerly exempt from licensing hours; a public house catering for such customers (from Latin 'in good faith').

A public-house ... humming with those whom Irish publicans are pleased to call 'Bona feeds' (Somerville and Ross).

'Not a decent house within four miles, the way [= so that] every living Christian is a bona fide' (Synge).

After closing time in the bona fides at the foot of the mountains (E. O'Brien).

bonav   Young pig (from Irish *banbh* /banəv/).

'He'd put the fear of death into the banbhs and the screeching sows' (Synge).

'Our bonavs dead! Our pigsty drenched with blood' (MacMahon).

bonnyclobber   Milk naturally clotted on souring (from Irish *bainne* /ban'ə/ = milk + gen. of *clábar* /kla:bər/ = mud). See also –>clabber.

The People live with Comfort on Potatoes and Bonnyclobber (Swift).

booley   Milking place in summer pasture; also 'bolly' et al. (from Irish *buaile* /buəl'ə/). 'Booleying' = transhumance.

Theare is one vse amongst them to keep theire Cattell and to live themselves the moste part of the year in <u>Bollyes</u> pasturing vppon the mountaine and waste wilde places and removinge still to freshe lande (Spenser).

Animals ... hidden in an upland booley (Kiely).

Achill was the last home of booleying (Evans).

Bord Fáilte The Tourist Board (from Irish *bord* /boːrd/ = board + *fáilte* /faːlˈtˈə/ = welcome).

Bord Failte doesn't tell visitors coming here to bring sunglasses in November (Binchy).

Bord na Móna The Peat Board (from Irish *bord* /boːrd/ = board + gen. of *móin* /moːnʲ/ = peat).

The landscape must have been ... busy in exactly the way it is today, with big Bord na Mona machines restlessly working the –>bog in the distance, and lots of contemporary road-making going on (Irish Times).

Bord Tráchtála The Board of Trade (from Irish *bord* /boːrd/ = board + gen. of *tráchtáil* /traːxtaːlʲ/ = trade).

'There is now a definite 'Irish factor' in Hollywood,' says Derry O'Brien of Bord Tráchtála's international services department (Irish Times).

boˈreen Lane, usually unmade and leading to a house (from Irish *bóthar* /boːhər/ = road + dimin.).

The finest dog fox you'd ever seen sailing ahead of them up the boreen (Boucicault).

I to whom Roman roads are a tedium / Preferring the boreens of a country / Rome never bothered her ponderous head about (MacNeice).

Even now, into December, the muddy verges of the boreens are pricked with startling new spears of green (Irish Times).

boˈstoon Lout (from Irish *bastún* /bastuːn/).

The incontinent bosthoons of his own class ... were seldom at large in this shabby quarter of the city (Beckett).

GLOSSARY

	'Are you the ignorant bostoon that's banging and hammering away at my knocker?' (D. Johnston).
bothered	Deaf (cf. Irish *bodhar* /baur/ = deaf).
	Bald Pat, bothered beetle, stands on the curbstone, folding his napkin, waiting to wait (Joyce).
	'Is it bothered as well as stupid you are?' (Brown).
bouchal	Boy, bachelor (from Irish *buachaill* /buəxəl'/).
	Tell me, tell me, Shawn O'Farrell, / Why it is you hurry so? / Hush <u>ma bouchal</u>, hush and listen, / And his cheeks were in a glow (Song).
bowsy	/bauzi/bu:zi/ Ruffian, boor.
	'–>Sure, amn't I never done at the drunken bowsy ever since he left school?' (Joyce).
	What a bowsy her ex-husband was (Durcan).
boxty	Bread, pancakes etc. made with potatoes (from Irish *bacstai* /baksti:/).
	The meals were the mashed potatoes referred to as –>pandy, potato bread or boxty (E. O'Brien).
	Boxty is another great Irish potato dish (Irish Times).
Brehon	Ancient Irish judge (from a form of Irish *breitheamh* /b'r'ehəv/, pl. *breithiúna* /b'r'ehu:nə/).
	[The Irish] haue allwaies preserued and kepte theire owne lawe which is the <u>Brehon</u> lawe (Spenser).
	Patsy Dan took on the title of king last year, fulfilling an historic role thought to have its tradition in the Brehon laws (Irish Times).
Brigid's Cross	Cross of rushes or straw woven annually on St. Bridget's

35

Eve, the last day of January, and believed to protect the household from fire and other harm.

Over the bed hangs a large St. Brigid's cross (J. B. Keane).

A Brigid's Cross / yellowing in some outhouse (Heaney).

brogue The marked dialectal accent with which English is spoken in Ireland; esp. formerly (cf. Irish *bróg* /bro:g/, shoe of untanned hide). See Introduction.

What we call the <u>Irish brogue</u> is no sooner discovered, than it makes the deliverer in the last degree ridiculous (Swift).

He exaggerated his native brogue (Edgeworth).

[Ireland's] children ... slouch around the world with a gesture and a brogue / And a faggot of useless memories (MacNeice).

brosna Kindling, faggots (from Irish *brosna* /brosnə/).

Dragged before the land-bailiff for daring to gather brosna in the woods (Corkery).

Old Dan Bride was breaking brosna for the fire (O'Connor).

broth of a boy The essence of what a boy should be. This became a popular Stage Irishism (see Appendix).

As he was a broth of a boy at dancing, the servants would strike up a dance in the kitchen (Carleton).

The famed British reserve is as much a myth as the idea of the broth-of-a-boy Irishman, he of the ready wit and the warm heart and the great love of a fight (Behan).

Brothers = –>Christian Brothers.

B-specials One of three categories of the all-Protestant Ulster Special Constabulary, established 1921, disbanded 1970.

A B-Special's hair had turned white (Montague).

[In the novel] the Mayo yeomanry are the shadowy and bigoted forerunners of the B Specials (Paulin).

buckeen Young man belonging to the inferior gentry (from 'buck' = fashionable young man + dimin.).

At Ennis ... there were of course the regular number of swaggering-looking buckeens (Thackeray).

The top-booted buckeen (W. Wilde).

bull Expression involving a ludicrous inconsistency unperceived by the speaker; often with the epithet 'Irish'.

From such a mouth, an Englishman expects nothing but bulls, blunders, and follies (Swift).

And how good of you ... in defiance of bulls and blunders, to allow us a comfortable English fireplace (Edgeworth).

'Nine o'clock mass will be held at ten o'clock. Is that an Irish bull?' (Tóibín).

Busaras /ˈbʌsaːrəs/ Bus station (from 'bus' + Irish *áras* /aːrəs/ = house, building).

He found himself walking eagerly towards the Busarus (McGahern).

cabin Cottage; the common word for the small houses or hovels lived in by Irish –>peasants.

The Streets, the Roads and Cabbin-doors crowded with Beggars of the Female Sex, followed by three, four, or six children, all in rags (Swift).

There was not a cabin at which he had not stopped ... to drink a glass of burnt whiskey out of an egg-shell (Edgeworth).

Roofs of abandoned cabins sag in slowly (Bowen).

cailleach Old woman, hag (from Irish *cailleach* /kal'əx/).

Beauty and peace I sing – / The fire on the open hearth, / The cailleach spinning at her wheel (Campbell).

I go to say goodbye to the <u>cailleach</u> / that terrible figure who haunted my childhood (Montague).

calcannon See –>colcannon.

call Claim, cause, right (same meaning as Irish *call* /kal/).

'What call has he to the mountain any more than I have?' (Kickham).

'You'll have no call to complain' (Synge).

This island to which ... he had no call to have come (J. O'Faolain).

caman Stick used in –>hurling (from Irish *camán* /kama:n/); also called a –>hurley.

'[He] made a woeful wipe at him one time with his caman' (Joyce).

camogie Women's game based on –>hurling (from Irish *camógaíocht* /kamo:gi:əxt/).

The ... county cup for camogie was left hanging in mid-air now that the ... captain in her green skirt had vanished (Bolger).

cannawan Bog-cotton (from Irish *ceannbhán* /k'anəva:n/).

As cheery as the springtime and as Irish as the cannawaun (Song).

Thy neck was, lost maid, / Than the <u>ceanabhan</u> whiter (Song).

GLOSSARY

carrageen An edible seaweed (from the name of a village west of Waterford); also called 'Irish moss'.

She'd pick her bag of carrageen (Synge).

She is remembered for having introduced piped icing, little scalloped roses and carrageen soufflés, into a bastion doggedly committed to potatoes and bacon and cabbage (E. O'Brien).

Castle Catholic Catholic who converted to Protestantism for material gain (Dublin Castle being the centre of British rule). See also next entry.

He was regarded by a great many people as a 'Castle Catholic' — a particularly detested breed in Ireland — and was considered a very fortunate man to get through the –>War of Independence with his life (Behan).

In this ... phantasmagoria Bloom becomes a castle Catholic and a voice calls him a 'turncoat' and reminds him that he once shouted 'Up the Boers!' (Paulin).

Castle hack Informer in the pay of Dublin Castle, the centre of British rule (cf. 'garrison-hack' = harlot). See also preceding entry.

'I believe half of them are in the pay of the Castle ... They're Castle hacks' (Joyce).

caubeen Old shabby hat or cap (from Irish *cáibín* /ka:b'i:n'/).

The primitive country-boys in caubeens, knee-breeches and green-tailed coats (Kiely).

I picture them, in their cawbeens and their shawls, straggling down the path to the beach (Banville).

causey See –>kesh.

cead mile failte The traditional Irish words of welcome (from Irish *céad*

/k'e:d/ = hundred + *míle* /m'i:l'ə/ = thousand + *fáilte* /fa:l't'ə/ = welcome).

[He] bid her a <u>cead mile failte</u>, just the same as if he had known her all his life (W. Wilde).

'Cead Mile Failte' said the President [i.e. Clinton], prompting another round of cheers and whoops (Irish Times).

ceanneasna Grey homespun (from Irish *ceanneasna* / k'anasnə/).

They were dressed in bainins [–>bawneen] and ceanneasna trousers (Macken).

ceili /k-/ Informal musical evening with songs and dancing (from Irish *céilí* /k'e:l'i:/ = friendly visit).

He could see them sweeping out the small hall where there would be a <u>ceili</u> tomorrow night (Macken).

On Sundays ... Rita went to a ceilidh (E. O'Brien).

Celtic Pertaining to the Celts. Nowadays usually pronounced /k-/, but /s-/ in names of football teams. See also next entry.

In his head still swirled the mists of Celtic legend (Flanagan).

Celtic Cross High carved stone cross with ring; found in early monastic settlements and much copied, esp. on Victorian tombstones. The term 'High Cross' is preferred by scholars.

Lambert said that the decorations on Celtic Crosses were probably derived from Coptic textiles (Longford).

A Celtic cross by the road commemorates no battle (R. Murphy).

The Celtic Cross is an extraordinary monument, towering twenty and more feet above us. It is made of massive stone blocks, and each of the four sides of each great block are

	carved into panels illustrating episodes from the Bible and the Apocrypha (Devlin).
cess	'Bad cess' = 'bad luck'. 'Cess' is perhaps from 'success', or from 'assessment', the term used in 16th century Ireland for money levied for the upkeep of military forces.

'The thousand militia — bad cess to them! — walking idle through the land' (Synge).

'–>Sure the –>Fenians is rightly dead and buried and bad cess to them for their mischief making' (Kilroy). |
| **chancer** | One who takes chances over-confidently; also used more generally as a term of contempt.

'Isn't he a sort of a bloody English chancer' (Murdoch).

'A chancer like that ... that gives a young fellow two-bob pieces' (Trevor). |
| **chaney** | = china. Also used in the plural.

'There was Molly cryin Me chaney, me beautyful chaney!' (Shaw).

Her brother had got the money from the savages for the trinkets and the chainies (Joyce). |
| **chapel** | Catholic place of worship, esp. formerly; Protestant places of worship were called 'churches'.

There was no human habitation within a circle of many miles, except the half-dozen hovels and the small thatched chapel composing the little village (Le Fanu).

The roads converging on chapels teem with people going to mass (Bowen). |
| **chassis** | = chaos.

'The whole worl's in a state o' chassis' (O'Casey). |

chiselur /tʃizələ/ Child. Also 'chiseller'.

'Chiselurs don't care a damn now about their parents' (O'Casey).

Us chisellers on the floor discussed the matter (Behan).

Christian Brothers Lay teaching order that dominated elementary teaching for generations. Also called merely 'The Brothers'.

The Christian Brothers did their best for him, and did it firmly, leather strap in hand, but, emerging wearily from –>penal laws and –>hedge-schoolmastering, had little time to mince round the fine arts (K. O'Brien).

Most of the people I had gone to school with were there ... and nearly all the Brothers who had taught us (McGahern).

CIE The national transport system (*córas* /ko:rəs/ = system + *iompair* /impər'/, gen. of *iompar* = transport + *Éireann* /e:r'ən/, gen. of –>*Éire*).

There had been three days of volunteer work trying to beautify the station. No money had been allotted by CIE, the railways company, for repainting (Binchy).

Cile See –>Sheela-na-Gig.

Citizen Army Militia founded in the interest of the trade union movement, committed to the nationalist cause in the –>Rising.

[He] saw a little bunch of people being hustled out of the Park by some of the Citizen Army (O'Duffy).

Civic Guards See –>Garda.

Civil War Warfare 1922-23 between supporters (–>Free Staters) and opponents (–>Republicans) of the Treaty with England signed in December 1921. See also –>Troubles.

There were some wild boys about there ... who were –>Irregulars; and they had slept and skirmished on the mountain-side in the Civil War (Longford).

	–>*Nineteen sixteen was mentioned all the time, and the* –>*Tan War as well, but not the Civil War* (Tóibín).
clabber	Mud (from Irish *clábar* /klaːbər/). See also –>bonnyclobber.
	The people were staring at my father, at the clabber on his boots and the wrinkles on his trousers (McLaverty).
	In the sucking clabber I would splash / Delightedly (Heaney).
clachan	Small village (from Irish *clochán* /kloxaːn/ = stepping stones, stone structure). See also –>clochaun.
	The clachan or hamlet, once the centre of communal life and tradition, is despised, a symbol of squabbling poverty (Evans).
	[The road in the hills] arrives at a neat little clachan of houses (Irish Times).
clarty	Dirty.
	'They're awful clarty people the French' (Reid).
class	Kind, sort.
	'Angel, that's a peculiar class of a name' (Behan).
	'He's the very class of fella I fair hate' (Molloy).
cleeve	Basket (from Irish *cliabh* /kˈlʲiəv/).
	Carrying a cleeve on his back (Synge).
	She was filling the 'cleeve' with big, round white cabbage heads (Fitzmaurice).
clevey	Shelf above a fireplace (from French *claveau* = lintel).

Her mother was glorifying the clevey with moitered paper of many colours, for Christmas was at hand (Fitzmaurice).

clochaun Small corbelled stone structure, nowadays used mainly for keeping pigs or poultry, or for storing milk etc. (from Irish *clochán* /kloxa:n/ = stepping stones, stone structure); also used of monastic –>beehive huts. See also –>clachan.

Another –>class of stone structure, allied to the clochaun in construction, is the stone sweat-house, the Irish version of the Turkish bath (Evans).

cloon Meadow (from Irish *cluain* /kluən'/).

Woodrow Wilson's homestead / in a cloon above Strabane (Paulin).

cnuceen Small hill (from Irish *cnoc* /knok/ + dimin.).

I went out on the cnuceen, a little hill between this cottage and the sea, to watch the people gathering –>carragheen moss (Synge).

Co = County (always placed before the proper name).

A business man accused of setting fire to his own hotel in Portrush, Co Antrim ... was yesterday freed on bail (Irish Times).

A Co Donegal farmer and his two sons gave evidence in the High Court yesterday (Irish Times).

codger Fellow (perhaps a variant of 'cadger' = scrounger, sponger).

He was a red-headed freckle-faced <u>codger</u> of about twenty years of age (W. Wilde).

coffin ship Overcrowded emigrant ship.

'Twenty thousand of them died in the coffinships' (Joyce).

Economic exigencies ... sent over a million people in coffin ships when a blight hit the potato crops in 1847 (E. O'Brien).

cog To cheat.

A story he told of two schoolboys whom their teacher suspected of cogging (Irish Times).

colcannon Dish of kale or white cabbage and potatoes, traditionally eaten at Halloween and often containing a lucky trinket (from Irish *cal ceann fhionn* /kal k'aun in/ = white-headed cabbage). Also 'kale-canon' et al.

'She'll get the ring –>itself in that helping of kale-canon' (Boucicault).

Colcannon means a different thing to people in different parts of the country. Some versions use kale, others cabbage, yet another includes parsnip (Irish Times).

colleen Young girl (from Irish *cailín* /kal'i:n'/). 'Colleen' is the common anglicised term, usually implying rural poverty and lack of sophistication.

'She is known at every fair and –>pattern in Munster as the Colleen –>Bawn' (Boucicault).

'A real Irish colleen. Never a shoe to her foot till the day she was married' (White).

come-all-you Street ballad (so called from its opening words).

Street singers, who sang a come-all-you about O'Donovan Rossa (Joyce).

The boys would take up an old come-all-ye (O'Nolan).

comether 'To put the comether on' is to beguile, to win over (from 'come' + 'hither').

'I wasn't long in putting my com'ether on her' (Trollope).

'She put the comether on him, sweet and twentysix' (Joyce).

conacre /kɔneikə/ The letting of small portions of land already tilled, for a short period and usually at a high rent (perhaps from 'corn' + 'acre').

Conacre (Title, Hewitt).

Potato land let in conacre, that is from year to year (Evans).

Congested District One of the very poorest parts of Ireland, which received Government assistance, esp. about 1900, through the Congested Districts Board.

He told me that Castle Carra had been sold to the Congested Districts Board (G. Moore).

Here in the congested districts of Mayo the land is still utterly insufficient (Synge).

The physical environment ... is only now recovering from the way it was stripped when it was a congested district (Irish Times).

coolun Fair maiden (from Irish *cúileann* /ku:l'ən/). 'The Coolun' is a well-known song.

'What makes you be shoving and moving your stool on / And singing all wrong that old song of The Coolun?' (Song).

'Then comes the siren with the black eyes, whose singing of the Coolin brought the tears to Mr. Kearney's eyes' (Kickham).

coppaleen Little horse (from Irish *capall* /kapəl/ + dimin.). Myles na gCopaleen /nə gopali:n/ (gen.pl. with mutation), 'Myles of the Little Horses', was a pen-name of Brian O'Nolan; the original Myles was a character in Boucicault's play *The –>Colleen –>Bawn* (1860).

'I saw your coppaleen beyant [= beyond] under the hedge' (Boucicault).

corner-boy   Rough who lounges about street corners.

A gang of corner-boys whose horse-play in the streets was the curse of the Ringsend district (O'Nolan).

No need for corner-boy language (Friel).

Count   Continental title often borne by members of the old Gaelic aristocracy who fled from Ireland after the Battle of Limerick 1691, to form Irish brigades and regiments on the Continent. See also –>wild geese.

The count was a fine old military-looking gentleman (Edgeworth).

Redmond, Count O'Hanlon, the Irish –>Rapparree (Title, Carleton).

court   –>Big House of great extent or beauty.

[He] had been at every –>bawne and coort in Connaught (W. Wilde).

Bowen's Court, finished in 1776, is a high bare Italianate house (Bowen).

crack   Lively talk; news; fun (spelt *craic* in Irish).

As soon as [the policeman] had turned the corner at the Cross Roads they streamed back into the pub to continue their crack (Devlin).

He wiped his nose with his hankie and got him to blow into it, and told him he'd have great crack picking the dried blood out of his nose (Doyle).

Few things are better craic than the mushroom hunts ... when the season comes round (Irish Times).

crane   Heron.

It's not for the common birds that I'd mourn, / The blackbird, the corn-crake or the crane (T. MacDonagh trans.).

> *The herons — called cranes by the country people — fish in the Funcheon* (Bowen).

crannog Lake-dwelling (from Irish *crannóg* /krano:g/).

> *I make my grove / on an old crannog* (Heaney).

> *She lived all alone in a crannóg / Which had an underwater zig-zag causeway* (Durcan).

cratur See –>creature.

creamery Factory for the processing of dairy produce.

> *The roads rattle with ass carts taking milk up to the creamery* (Bowen).

> *I saw my father come on a tractor, two creamery cans on the trailer* (McGahern).

creature Term of commiseration, 'poor thing'; also spelt 'cratur' et al.

> *'The pig –>itself – the cratur – skreetching alive wid [= with] the hunger'* (Hall).

> *Peter's wife was very sorry at my going, the creature* (Iremonger trans.).

> *She was always referred to as the Creature by the townspeople* (E. O'Brien).

creepie Low stool.

> *Drawing his 'creepie' closer to the fire* (Hall).

> *The favourite fireside stool was the three-legged creepie* (Evans).

cromlech /krɔmlək/ Ancient prehistoric structure consisting of a large flat stone laid across two or more other stones standing upright (from Welsh). See also –>dolmen.

We who still labour by the cromlech on the shore (Yeats).

They went on wandering after that, all through Ireland, hiding from Fionn in every place, sleeping under cromlechs or with no shelter at all (Kiely).

croppy Nickname for the rebels of 1798, who wore close-cropped hair.

We'll fight for our country, our king, and his crown, / and make all the traitors and croppies lie down (Song).

Requiem for the Croppies (Title, Heaney).

crow Often = rook.

The melodious cawing of the crows in Squire Grimshaws's rookery (Carleton).

[He] had heard now and again of a –>garden ruined by crows (Fitzmaurice).

cruach Stack, pile (from Irish *cruach* /kruəx/).

The sudden downpour of rain towards the end of August swept his newly-gathered cruach of –>turf from the –>inches (Corkery).

crubeen Pig's foot (from Irish *crúbín* /kru:b'i:n'/).

Applewomen and vendors of 'crubeens', <u>alias</u> pig's feet, a grisly delicacy peculiar to Irish open-air holiday-making (Somerville and Ross).

Florence MacCabe takes a crubeen and a bottle of double X for supper every Saturday (Joyce).

cruiskeen Small jug (from Irish *crúiscín* /kru:s'ki:n'/). 'The Cruiskeen Lawn' (Irish *lán* = full) is a well-known drinking song.

I, more blest than they, / Spend each night and happy day, / With my smilin' little Cruiskeen Lawn, Lawn, Lawn (Song).

'There he is ... in his gloryhole, with his cruiskeen lawn and his load of papers, working for the cause' (Joyce).

The cruiskín sign above the entrance [of a distillery] (Egan).

culchie   Contemptuous term for a countryman (allegedly from the name of a village in County Mayo, Kiltimagh or *Coillte Mách*).

'It's easy knowing the Culchies never saw a queue. All they know is pushin' and shovin'' (Iremonger trans.).

The Culchiemachs, as we call the Irish speaking people (Behan).

Culdee   Member of an ancient religious order, found from the eighth century (from Old Irish *céle dé* = servant of God).

The Culdees knew each –>drumlin (Clarke).

The quatrains on Aengus the Culdee (O'Connor).

cumann   (Branch of an) association (from Irish *cumann* /kumən/). Found in the names of many organisations, e.g. *Cumann na mBan* /kumən nə man/ = The Women's Association.

'It is an honour for me, as chairman of this Enniscorthy cumann of –>Fianna Fáil, to introduce a young man who hails from one of the –>Republican families of this town' (Tóibín).

curate   Grocer's or publican's assistant.

The curate served. — 'How much is that?' (Joyce).

He had heard from a messenger sent by a curate, i.e., assistant in the pub-cum-grocery, that two suspicious characters had been seen (Kiely).

He ... pushed open a door, and lifted a finger to a white-coated curate (White).

currach /kʌrə(x)/ Light sea-going rowing-boat, formed of cow hides or pitched cloth stretched on a frame of wicker-work (from Irish *curach* /kurəx/). Also spelt 'cur(r)agh'.

The three young men who fished in the same curragh with him and were his bosom friends (O'Flaherty).

The other currachs were far out in the bay already (Lavin).

Curragh /kʌrə/ Area in County Kildare with many establishments for breeding and training horses; the centre of Irish racing. Also the site of a military camp (cf. Irish *curchas* = marsh).

Every one wore a tall silk hat at the Curragh in the seventies (G. Moore).

He could talk of nothing but race-horses and his ambition to breed them at the curragh (K. O'Brien).

Recently released from the internment camp on the Curragh of Kildare, famous for horses, short grass, sheep, soldiers and internees, he said he was feeling better after a holiday in Connemara (Kiely).

cute Sharp, intelligent (abbr. of 'acute').

'He was always a smart, active, 'cute boy' (Croker).

He shakes several hands. Being Irish country-cute they are well aware that he's boozed (Kiely).

The Opposition is getting cuter ... [It] can't succeed in the –>Dail. But there is still the odd fast one it can pull (Irish Times).

Dáil Éireann /da:l' e:r'ən/ The Lower House of the Irish Parliament, often called merely 'The Dáil'.

'There are going to be questions in the Dail if the Institute uses public money to put out political propaganda' (White).

By news she did not mean the happenings in Dail Eireann or on the stock exchange (Boylan).

It seemed only a matter of time before he was elected to the Dáil (McGahern).

Danaan Fairy (referring to the *Tuatha De Danaan*, the Tribes of the goddess Dana or Danu, who were traditionally masters of magic).

I am haunted by numberless islands, and many a Danaan shore (Yeats).

dander To walk about in a leisurely way.

They dandered along past by where the empty vehicle was waiting (Joyce).

'I was dandering by / and says I, I might as well call' (Heaney).

dark Sometimes = blind. See also —>black.

'Asking the way of an old dark fiddler, and him tip-tapping (D. Johnston)

The blind Man / Dark from birth / And therefore spared the shock / Of losing light (Kennelly).

DART = Dublin Area Rapid Transit: an electric rail service operating from Dublin north to Howth and south to Bray.

'I met him on the DART there yesterday' (Doyle).

Travelling by DART is a nice experience, far more comfortable than than taking the Paris Metro or the London tube (Irish Times).

deeshy Very small.

'A little deeshy grass-hopper' (Shaw).

delft Porcelain, crockery; also 'delph', 'delf'.

Packing our cracked delf tea and dinner services in a basket (Le Fanu).

'This is plundering a whole estate. Cattle, horse, sheep, pigs ... The furniture, pictures, the delph, glassware' (Behan).

The delft horseshoe of the lavatory bowl (MacLaverty).

demesne /diˈmein/ The land immediately attached to a mansion (from Latin *dominicus* = belonging to a lord); also 'domain'.

English people ... say 'park' where we say 'demesne' (Bowen).

The crumbling domain wall ... seemed like a natural excrescence (Murdoch).

The castle burned in the early 19th century and the family abandoned the ruin, eventually building a new house elsewhere in the demesne (Irish Times).

deputy Title of a –>Teachta Dáilí or –>TD.

Deputy Austin Currie, and indeed –>Fine Gael in general, were saved from a major embarassment last weekend (Irish Times).

diamond In the north of Ireland: town square.

Old people ... rested without words, under the protection of the Virgin Victory, on seats in the Diamond (Kiely).

Diehard Member of –>Republican forces opposed to the –>Treaty of 1922; an –>Irregular.

'Everybody's sayin' that he was a diehard' (O'Casey).

dilisk See –>dulse.

dispossess To put out of possession; esp. with reference to the Irish driven from their lands by waves of invaders.

Ireland was never fully taken, though most thoroughly dispossessed (E. O'Brien).

The hermits, fiercely dispossessed, / Found refuge among gulls and rocks (Montague).

A great estate given to an English family ... who collected rents and dues until the land was ceded back to the descendants of the earlier dispossessed (Devlin).

ditch Dyke or raised bank. What is known as a 'ditch' in England — an open drain along a bank or road — is usually called the '–>gripe of the ditch' in Ireland, or a '–>sheugh' in the northern parts of the country.

His house was approached by a deep narrow –>boreen, generally so wet and muddy that one had to walk on the top of the ditch on either side more frequently, than traverse the gully beneath (W. Wilde).

Looking over a low ditch or a high ditch (Synge).

divil = devil (often pronounced /divəl/, esp. when used as a mild imprecation); 'devil a'/'divil a' = 'not a'.

'What! ... No sheets?' 'Divil a sheet' (Lover).

'London is I believe full of good pictures, divil a one have I seen as yet' (Ross).

dolmen French name for –>cromlech.

Like dolmens round my childhood, the old people (Montague).

Less than a mile over the fields was one of the best-preserved dolmens in the country (Brady).

domain See –>demesne.

Donnybrook A notorious fair formerly held at Donnybrook near Dublin, which became synonymous with a brawl or free fight. As adj.: boisterous, swaggering.

> *Prentiss and his mother had watched a scuffle from the tall windows of the Imperial Hotel ... 'There you are,' one of the other ladies had said to his mother, 'the country turned into a Donnybrook'* (Flanagan).

> *'He did have the cockiness of your typical Donnybrook Irishman'* (Kilroy).

dotey Term of endearment, esp. to a child.

> *'Ask me nicely, Hickey, and call me dotey.' 'Dotey. Ducky. Darling. Honeybunch, do you want a white or brown egg for your breakfast?'* (E. O'Brien).

dozy Sleepy; stupid.

> *Everyone forgot about Fred, the dozy bull in the next field ... after the fertility dance Fred, the bull, suddenly developed a crush on cows* (Kiely).

> *Goodbye to the humble little mounds, the ragwort, the chicken runs, the dozy hens* (E. O'Brien).

drisheen Pudding made from blood stuffed into the intestines of a sheep (from Irish *drisín* /d'r'is'i:n'/).

> *Mr Dedalus had ordered drisheens for breakfast* (Joyce).

drumlin Small rounded hill formed by glacial drift (cf. Irish *droim* /drom'/ = back, ridge).

> *This is drumlin country, of course: a long parade of grassy, whale-backed hillocks* (Irish Times).

dudeen Short-stemmed clay pipe (from Irish *dúidín* /du:d'i:n'/.

> *'First let me light my doodeen'* (Hall).

> *Standing there at the counter with his old dudeen in his mouth and talking away in Irish* (Iremonger trans.).

dulse	/dʌls/ An edible reddish-brown seaweed; also 'dilisk' et al. (from a variant of Irish *duileasc* /dil'əsk/). |//

dulse   /dʌls/ An edible reddish-brown seaweed; also 'dilisk' et al. (from a variant of Irish *duileasc* /dil'əsk/).

'A place where periwinkles are plenty, and there is dilisk thrown in heaps' (Fitzmaurice).

The sugar was tastefully disguised under a top-dressing of dulse (Kiely).

dun   Ancient hill fortress (from Irish *dún* /du:n/ = fort, promontory).

Grania begins to speak of Finn ... her object being to persuade Diarmuid to invite Finn to his dun (G. Moore).

One of the largest Duns, or pagan forts, on the islands, is within a stone's throw of my cottage (Synge).

Easter Week   Easter 1916, which saw the armed Rising in Dublin.

'The bullet he got in Easter Week was bad enough' (O'Casey).

One minute, there's a tear-jerker about Easter Week, the next we have reminiscences about the playing fields of Eton [said of radio programmes] (Irish Times).

Easter Lily   Daffodil (sold at Easter to commemorate the Easter Rising in 1916).

I bought an Easter Lily on the bridge (Iremonger trans.).

eejit   = idiot, reflecting a common pronunciation. Also 'iijit'.

There was another half-eejit that had just arrived over from County Derry (Iremonger trans.).

There'll always be some eejit left to sound <u>The Last Post</u> (McGahern).

A flash and the motorised ejection whirr of the Polaroid startled Minogue. He had been leaning on the button. Iijit (Brady).

GLOSSARY

Éire /eːrˈə/ The Irish name of Ireland, which appears in Old Irish texts as 'Eriu', the name of a queen in Irish mythology. In the Irish Constitution of 1937, *Éire* (in the English language: *Ireland*) replaced the name –>*Saorstát Éireann* (in the English language: the –>*Irish Free State*).

She chanted me a chant, a beautiful and grand hymn, / Of him who should be shortly Éire's reigning king (Mangan trans.).

I would, before my time to go, / Sing of old Eire and the ancient ways (Yeats).

'Ah,' [said the man at the Labour Exchange in Belfast], 'you're birds of passage from Eire,' but he pronounced it Ayr. 'Ayr,' says I, 'is in Scotland' (Behan).

elk The so-called 'Irish Elk' is really a giant deer, known only from remains found in the bogs.

On one side of the lofty and spacious hall stood the skeleton of an elk (Edgeworth).

They've taken the skeleton / Of the Great Irish Elk (Heaney).

emerald 'The Emerald Isle' is a name for Ireland, coined about 1800 by William Drennan.

Nor one feeling of vengeance presume to defile / The cause, or the men, of the Emerald Isle (Drennan).

In the grand Allan liner we're sailin' in style / But we're sailing away from the Emerald Isle (French).

Emergency 'The Emergency' was the period of the Second World War, during which Ireland remained neutral.

During the Emergency, when cigarettes will be scarce and rationed (Higgins).

All through the war years, or the Emergency as it was called, they had travelled down from Dublin on a train fuelled by –>turf (Binchy).

emergency man
Bailiff's officer recruited for a special purpose, esp. in evictions.

The door was closed and barred but it was easily smashed in by the emergency men (MacBride).

'Twenty years ago they sent down a 'mergency man to ... serve processes on the people' (Synge).

entirely
Intensifier (placed at the end of a phrase); formerly often spelt 'intirely' (see Introduction).

'Isn't it a cruel thing entirely' (Boucicault).

'She's very bad intirely, ma'am' (Trollope).

'You were a foolish man entirely not to tell me about this letter' (Brady).

Erin
Ancient name for Ireland (from inflected form of *Ériu*, modern –>*Éire*).

Yet still in her darkness doth Erin lie sleeping, / Still doth the pure light its dawning delay (T. Moore).

'At sunset, when one got maudlin and called Ireland Erin' (Shaw).

Erse
The ancient Celtic language of Scotland and Ireland. The name is not preferred by Irish speakers to-day.

'The moment I heard the Erse I knew you boys were straight' (Plunkett).

'Irish?' said Mrs. Pybus. 'Not Erse?' – 'Irish,' said Lambert. 'Gaelic' (Longford).

ESB
= Electricity Supply Board.

The grey-haired man was a bachelor, employed in the ESB (Trevor).

There was no one looking after the E.S.B. pylon depot so we climbed in (Doyle).

esker	Ridges of post-glacial gravel (from Irish *eiscir* /es'k'ər'/).
	A spine of sandy, heathery esker-land where once the glaciers had stopped (Kiely).
	Who owns the land where musket-balls are buried / In blackthorn roots on the eskar? (R. Murphy).
faction fight	Hand-to-hand fighting between groups of –>peasants, often at fairs and similar gatherings.
	O'Carroll .. was a notorious faction fighter and therefore suspect as a –>Whiteboy (Flanagan).
	'In the faction fighting times, several were killed there' (Molloy).
fáinne	Plain gold ring worn as a lapel pin by Irish speakers (from Irish *fáinne* /fa:n'ə/ = ring).
	He was a fluent speaker of Irish and wore the gold fáinne in the lapel of his jacket (Plunkett).
	A teacher, the gold fáinne and metal –>tricolour in his lapel (McGahern).
faith	Mild expletive.
	'I never saw you before.' 'Faith, then you'll never see me agin [= again]' (Lover).
	'He's writing a book about the Fitzgeralds he told me. He's well up in history, faith' (Joyce).
faix	Mild expletive (from 'faikins': 'fay' or 'faith' + dimin. '-kins').
	'He's going ... with two young ladies.' 'Oh! –>be-gorra ... and so he is; and, faix, ye might do worse' (Lever).
	'You're jokin' sure.' 'Faix, it's no joke' (Lover).
Famine	Usually = the Great Famine of the 1840s.

GLOSSARY

It was he who reared the large obelisk in front of the Grand Lodge, as a piece of –>relief work during the Famine (Longford).

'I think the Famine and the emigration has done the country more good than harm' (Kilroy).

famine road Road (often leading nowhere) built under the relief scheme set up by the Government to provide employment for the poor during periods of famine, esp. in the 1840s.

Barren, never to know the load / of his child in you, what is your body / now if not a famine road? (Boland).

farl Thin oatmeal cake; orig. = quarter section of round cake (contr. of 'fardel' from OE *féorða dǽl* = fourth part).

–>Soda farls, strong tea, / New rope, rock salt, kale plants, / Potato bread and Woodbine (Heaney).

His mother stood at the range making –>soda farls (Laverty).

FÁS /fa:s/ The Training and Employment Authority: *Foras* /forəs/ = authority + *Áiseanna* /a:s'ənə/ = services + *Saothair* /se:hər'/, gen. = of *saothar* labour, 'The labour services authority'. *Fás* is also an Irish word meaning 'growth', 'development'.

FÁS scheme aims to benefit nearly 150,000 jobless (Headline, Irish Times).

fear an tí /f'ar ə(n) t'i:/ = 'man of the house'; master of ceremonies.

As fear an tí, Mick Lally will juggle with the considerable talents and achievements of Tommy Hayes ... (Irish Times).

feck To steal (variant of English thieves' slang 'fake' = to rob; of obscure origin).

'Do you think you could contribute half-a-crown?' 'I could feck it, I suppose.' Dick raised his eyelashes. 'Feck?'

	Gong Gong looked shamedly at the tiles. 'I mean steal,' he whispered (S. O'Faolain).
feish	Festival (from Irish *feis* /f'es'/). 'Feis Cheoil' /f'es' xo:l'/ = Festival of Music (*feis* + gen. of *ceol* = music).
	Race days, big matches and feishes bring all the hired cars out (Bowen).
	Mr Bell, the second tenor, was a fair-haired little man who competed every year for prizes at the Feis Ceoil (Joyce).
	I courted Maureen Canavan after a feis in Ballygawley, kissing and fondling on a low bridge opposite the –>RUC –>barracks (Montague).
Fenian	Member of republican organisation, the Fenians, founded 1858 (so named in honour of the ancient –>Fianna).
	[Home Rule is] very much less bloody than Fenianism (Trollope).
	He came from a rotten family, drunks and Fenians all (M. Keane).
	'Give us a rebel song, Mrs. Grunt, ma'm, a real Fenian one' (Behan).
Fianna	/f'iənə/ Legendary band of warriors in Ancient Ireland, adopted in the names of several modern organisations. See next and preceding entry.
	Unfinished dreams / Are buried with the Fianna / In that remote rock cave (Montague).
	Another history test [at school] — the life of the Fianna (Doyle).
Fianna Fáil	= 'Soldiers of Destiny' (from Irish fianna /f'iənə/ = warriors + gen. of *fál* /fa:l/ = destiny). One of the two major parties in Irish politics, the other being –>Fine Gael. See preceding entry.

Fianna Fail and Labour Party negotiators have agreed (Irish Times).

file Poet in Ancient Ireland (Irish *file* /fˈilˈə/, pl. *filí*).

The feats of memorisation of the <u>filí</u> of yore (Irish Times).

Fine Gael = 'Tribe of the Gaels' (from Irish *fine* /fˈinˈə/ = tribe + gen. pl. of –>*gael* /geːl/). One of the two major parties in Irish politics, the other being –>Fianna Fáil.

The Fine Gael leader ... was quick to his feet after the –>Taoiseach announced the business (Irish Times).

Firbolg One of the early mythical inhabitants of Ireland.

[The statue] was a Firbolg in the borrowed cloak of a –>Milesian (Joyce).

[The –>Formorians] were invaded and ousted by the Firbolgs, the men of the paunchy stomachs who came from Greece (E. O'Brien).

flahool Generous (from Irish *flaithiúil* /flahuːlˈ/).

All I could see was a poor middle-aged woman ... dressed in the cast-off hat and coat of some <u>flahool</u> old one [–>ould] she'd be doing a day's work for (Behan).

It was a flahool household and the liquor flowed free (J. B. Keane).

flying column Full-time mobile section, the principal unit used by the –>IRA in the –>War of Independence.

A number of flying columns, able to retire out of the city if necessary, would do the enemy more damage (Murdoch).

'I'll remember it ... the way old men in the country remember the flying column and the ambush against the –>Black and Tans' (White).

Fomorians Mythical early inhabitants of Ireland; also 'Formorians' (cf. Irish *fomhórach* /fovo:rəx/ = pirate, giant).

'There is little that has happened in West Cork since the days of the ancient Fomorians that isn't stuck away somewhere [in my mind]' (Flanagan).

Formorian fierceness of family and local feud (Montague).

fooster To be flurried, to fuss (from Irish *fústar* /fu:stər/ = fuss).

'I wonder what is he foostherin' for now?' (O'Casey).

He just foosthered around the place when there was anything to be done (Kilroy).

footless Senseless from drink.

[He] was never as footless as Pitt (Behan).

'You and I are going to get footless drunk' (Friel).

Formorian See –>Fomorian.

forenent Opposite. Also 'forenint' et al.

'The place forenent the grate [= great] gate would be quite the thing' (Hall).

'Her mother's grave was forenint the spot' (Boucicault).

frahan See –>frocan.

frawhawn See –>frocan.

Free Stater One who accepted the status of Free State for Ireland. See also –>Irish Free State and –>Civil War.

In 1921 came the –>Treaty, to be followed by the disintegration of Civil War — the dissentients to the Treaty,

–>*Republicans, in arms against the Free Staters who had accepted it* (Bowen).

–>*Republicans and Free Staters were waging civil war* (O'Flaherty).

frieze Coarse woollen cloth formerly used for men's clothes in the country (from French).

The young men wore corduroy trousers and frieze coats, the old men were still in knee breeches and tall hats (G. Moore).

Both wore the loose white frieze shirt that Inverara –>peasants use for work in the fields (O'Flaherty).

frocan Bilberry (from Irish *fraochán* /fre:xa:n/fri:xa:n/). Also 'frahan', 'frawhawn'.

In summer we have the best frawhawns in all the country (Swift).

Some little boys were returning from a ramble through the dark and devious –>glen ... with their pockets laden with nuts and 'frahans' (Le Fanu).

Marshy ground too poor to bear anything but heather and reeds and an odd cluster of purple frocans (Plunkett).

furze The common word in Ireland for the prickly bush *Ulex europæus*; also –>'gorse', 'whin'.

Surrounding the furze, they drove the rabbits this way and that (G. Moore).

I found you dead before me / Beside a little furze-bush (Dillon trans.).

GAA = The Gaelic Athletic Association, founded 1884 to preserve and popularise the native Irish pastimes of –>hurling, –>Gaelic football, and –>handball.

The scheme ... has added to the image of the GAA and its games and has attracted countrywide interest (Irish Times).

	Charlie Redmond's penalty kick and Neil Collins' save have already become the stuff of GAA legend and will be the subject of debate in the long nights after –>Samhain (Irish Times).
Gael	Irishman or Irishwoman (Irish *gael* /geːl/, from Old Irish *goídel*); often contrasted with –>Gall. See also next entries.
	'The Gods of the Gael have never spoken in the English language ' (G. Moore).
	And what to me is Gael or –>Gall? / Less than the Latin or the Greek (Colum).
Gaelic	Sometimes used of the three Celtic languages of Scotland, Ireland and Man; now chiefly = Scottish Gaelic. Gaelic is also used of the culture associated with the Irish language. See section on The Two Languages in Ireland.
	The Scotchmen shouted out to each other in Gaelic, the coarse and barbarous Gaelic of the Highlands, which the Kerrymen could but half understand (Flanagan).
	He traces the forging of this cultural nationalism in the 19th century through the unearthing of the lost Gaelic past (McGahern).
Gaelic football	Game popular all over Ireland, based on an ancient Irish game; superficially like a blend of rugby and association football. See –>GAA.
	At school they played Gaelic football (Kiely).
	'He sincerely believes that our forefathers wore kilts and played Gaelic football when they weren't writing –>Aislings' (Plunkett).
Gaelic League	Organisation devoted to the Irish language and the preservation of native culture, founded 1893. See section on The Two Languages in Ireland.
	These –>bog-trotters of Gaelic Leaguers (S. O'Faolain).

He stared sadly at the dusky, sweet-smelling fields which were a small part of the Ireland only he and the Gaelic League knew how to love (Plunkett).

Gaeltacht Irish-speaking district (from Irish *gaeltacht* /ge:ltəxt/). See –>Galltacht and section on The Two Languages in Ireland.

It's in English their family will be reared, even if they themselves speak the old tongue, as a lot of the Gaeltacht people here [i.e. in England] do (Iremonger trans.).

I knew this place well, / –>kelp on the stones, oh yes — /... Yes, these, the old hills, now made of Irish tweed: / I know this Gaeltacht well (Hartnett).

Peggy, a native Irish speaker from the Donegal Gaeltacht (Daly).

gaffer (Young) fellow (perhaps from 'godfather').

'Ten thousand blessings upon all that's here, for you've turned me a –>likely gaffer in the end of all' (Synge).

'They wanted some innocuous gaffer to look in on some goings-on here' (Brady).

gale Rent paid at a fixed interval (perhaps from OE *gafol* = tribute). 'Hanging gale' is rent due at a previous rent-day.

Hand over ... your accounts, with the balance due of the <u>hanging gale</u> (Edgeworth).

'The last gale to your lordship – and we never pay that till next May' (Trollope).

Gall A non-Irish person (from Irish *gall* /gal/ = foreigner). Often used of English and other invaders, and contrasted with –>Gael.

Whether –>Gael or Gall, there was not a –>big house in Ireland that did not rule as well as manage its own –>domain (Corkery).

'You do not hear the muffled call, / The sword being forged, the far-off tread / Of hosts to meet as –>Gael and Gall' (Colum).

gallous Fine, spirited, smart (orig. = villainous, fit for the gallows).

'There's a great gap between a gallous story and a dirty deed' (Synge).

'Gallous garage they have there' (Beckett).

gallowglass Mercenary soldier of Irish-Scandinavian ancestry (from Irish *gallóglach* /galo:gləx/).

He met the Travelling Gunman / instead of the Gallowglass (Hewitt).

'Didn't your great Prince O'Donnell come raging through here with his –>kernes and gallowglasses at the time of the great rebellion' (Flanagan).

Galltacht English-speaking district (from Irish *galltacht* /galtəxt/; cf. *gall* = foreigner). A term used occasionally in contrast to –>Gaeltacht; see also –>Gall.

galore Enough, plenty (from Irish *go leor* /gə l'o:r/).

There was Pat Kenessy's tent, with a green flag flowing without and whisky 'gilloure' flowing within (Hall).

With debts galore, but fun far more; / Oh, that's 'the man for Galway' (Lever).

gansey Knitted vest or shirt, generally of a type worn by seamen (from a variant of the name Guernsey, one of the Channnel Islands).

His shoulders were very broad and his chest was pressing tightly against the blue gansie he was wearing (Macken).

'Not a top-coat to him, the shirt neck open, nor a gansey' (T. Murphy).

gap

Hole in a hedge or wall, sometimes filled in with available materials.

One of those erections pleasantly termed 'gaps' in Ireland. On this occasion the gap was made of three razor-edged slabs of slate leaning against an iron bar (Somerville and Ross).

He looks at a page as a mule balks at a gap (R. Murphy).

garda

Policeman (Irish /ga:rdə/, pl. *gardaí* /ga:rdi:/. Also used in the English form 'guard', pl. 'guards'). The Irish Police Force is called the *Gardaí Siochána* /ga:rdi: s'i:xa:nə/ = Guardians of the Peace, also known as 'Civic Guards'.

'The Civic Guards had to break in, or the police it was then' (Longford).

The two guards left the –>barracks at ten past four (J. Johnston).

One of the Gardai studying the licence number of a parked car (E. O'Brien).

Narrow worlds dominated by the local priest, schoolmaster and Garda (Irish Times).

garden

Often = potato patch.

The tailor owed a small trifle of arrear of rent for his potato-garden (Trollope).

The garden where the –>praties grow (Song).

garron

Small and inferior kind of Irish or Scottish horse (from Irish *gearrán* /g'ara:n/). Also 'garraun' et al.

'–>Sure it isn't such a garron as that you'd put before his honour?' (Hall).

The Royal Canal packet-boat, dragged by a pair of lazy garrauns at the rate of three miles an hour (W. Wilde).

Not a prancing, restless, giggling, sideway-going, useless garran, but an animal well made, well bitted, with perfect paces (Trollope).

gas Jape, gossip.

The sisters would sit on the tiny patch of lawn at the back of the house, shelling peas and having a great old gas (Lewis).

'It was only a bit of gas' (Behan).

gassan See –>gossoon.

gawbeen Dull, stupid fellow, blockhead (from Irish *gáibín* /ga:b'i:n'/).

'I'm damned if I'll go on letting those gawbeens in here' (J. Johnston).

gauger Exciseman; one who assesses ('gauges') contents of barrels, etc.

'A primitive still, which I've just caught out yonder in the –>bog; and I'm carrying it in with all speed to the gauger' (Edgeworth).

Hughie brought to the light a bottle of white spirits that had never known gauger (Kiely).

geasa /g'asə/ Taboos, often laid on warriors in heroic literature (from Irish pl. of *geis* /g'es'/).

The new geasa that were laid on Cuchulain were that he should not go forth alone (O'Duffy).

He had had the ill luck ... to break all his geasa or taboos (Kiely).

gentleman 'The gentleman that pays the rent' was a facetious reference to a pig, esp. in 19th century English humour. For spellings 'jintleman', 'gintleman' see Introduction.

'I'm takin the gintleman that pays the rint for a dhrive' (Shaw).

'I am proud to be associated with the jintleman that pays the rint. I drink to the decent Irish pig' (White).

gilloure　　　See –>galore.

gilly　　　/g-/ Servant (from Irish *giolla* /g'ilə/).

A blacksmith ... was at work with a rough gilly to help him (Thackeray).

I am the gilly of Christ, / The mate of Mary's son; / I run the roads at seeding time / And when the harvest's done (Campbell).

'[Gilchrist] is an old Irish name. In its original form "Giolla Christ", the servant or gilly of the Lord.' 'You're a –>quare-looking gilly of the lord, you whore' (Behan).

gintleman　　　See –>gentleman.

girsha　　　Young girl (from Irish *girseach* /g'irs'əx/).

'Don't be so hard on yourself, girsha' (Kilroy).

glaur　　　Watery mud (from Irish *glár* /gla:r/); 'glaury' as adj.

The plaiting thorns / Have not been bill-hooked back / And a thick glaur floats (Montague).

Mould is relatively clean and thin, –>clabber is thick and dirty, and glaur is the ultimate — an oozing heavy wetness that clings to all the many extremeties of child and beast (Devlin).

The glaury sticky grave (Egan).

glen　　　Narrow lonely valley (from Irish *gleann* /g'l'an/).

In these glens many women still wear old-fashioned bonnets, with a frill round the face (Synge).

Though John Redney's house was far back in the glen, his straggling farm spread out into the river valley of which the glen itself was, as one might say, a side pocket, narrow and secret (Corkery).

By the wrongs we suffered / in that long twilight over –>bog and glen (Hewitt).

glib   Shaggy mass of hair hanging over the eyes (from Irish *glib* /g'l'ib'/). An early attribute of the Stage Irishman (see Appendix).

They haue another Custome ... that is the wearinge of mantells [= mantles] and long glibbes which is a thick Curled bushe of haire hanginge downe over theire eyes (Spenser).

Glibs of hanging hair blinding them (Kiely).

gob   Mouth (from Irish *gob* /gob/ = beak, mouth).

The farmer was gob-open (S. O'Faolain).

'I'll break your bloody gob, O'Shea, if you don't quit [= stop] shoving' (Brown).

gobshite   Worthless fool (from preceding entry + –>shite).

'They were a venomous pack of jolter-headed [= block-headed] gobshites' (T. Murphy).

'This King and Queen stuff is for children. Or gobshites' (Brady).

gombeen   Exploiting, untrustworthy dealer (from Irish *gaimbín* /gam'b'i:n'/ = exorbitant interest); also 'gombeen-man'.

'Dean Swift ... could tell one madman from another just as he could tell one gombeen from another' (E. O'Brien).

Behind a web of bottles, bales, / Tobacco, sugar, coffin nails / The gombeen like a spider sits, / Surfeited (Campbell).

The land now gone to gombeen men and compulsory purchase (Banville).

gorse Generally, a common prickly bush with yellow flowers, *Ulex europæus*; see –>furze. 'Gorse' may also be used more broadly to include i.a. heather.

The distant mountains ... Purple patched in summer with the purple, tough-rooted gorse (Flanagan).

gossoon Little boy, often one employed as a messenger; also 'gassan' (Irish spelling *garsún*; from French *garçon*).

The little <u>gossoon</u> was sent off to the neighbours to ... beg or borrow some [–>turf] (Edgeworth).

'*Even if they <u>are</u> barefooted gassans at least they're young hardy chaps*' (Kavanagh).

'*Your great and noble grand-father, the Captain, that employed a hundred men and more gossoons*' (Longford).

goster Gossip, idle talk (cf. the Irish phrase *gasrán cainte* = conversation). Also verb.

He was leaning on the counter in his shirt sleeves having a deep goster with Alderman Cowley (Joyce).

'*I've no time to stand here gostherin' with you*' (O'Casey).

'*A couple of men to be gostering and making chatter about the trouble and misfortune tormenting a poor old woman*' (D. Johnston).

GPO = General Post Office. The GPO in Dublin's Sackville Street (now O'Connell Street) was the headquarters of the Rising in 1916, and the scene of the insurgents' last stand.

'*I hear they're blazing away out o' th' G.P.O.*' (O'Casey).

Collins never wanted to re-enact the Greek tragedy of the GPO again (Jordan).

grabber Landgrabber; one who takes a farm from which a tenant has been evicted.

'You won't free Ireland by sending over the occasional lad to put a bullet in a grabber' (Flanagan).

grah Love, liking (from Irish *grá* /gra:/). See also –>agra.

'I hope ... it's not for her money that you have any grah for her' (Carleton).

'I think Bridge had a grah for me all along' (Fitzmaurice).

graip Dung fork (cf. Danish *greb*).

'You'd get a false kick or a prod of a graip' (Kavanagh).

'Once with a pitchfork Doran drove the four police out of the –>barracks in the village.' 'It was a graip. Your father misinformed you' (Kiely).

great Sometimes = on very friendly terms.

'I was great with him at that time,' she said (Joyce)

'Eleven years I'm great to Julia' (Molloy).

These days she was great with young Niall, and already the boy was beginning to look the better for it (Binchy).

gripe Trench, generally beside a high –>ditch or fence.

Leaping across the –>ditch, or, as he called it, the <u>gripe</u> of the –>ditch (Edgeworth).
Jamesie got out of the cold, shallow gripe, straightened himself up, and looked blinkingly at the river (Fitzmaurice).

'Give me your hand and I'll give you a pull over that gripe' (Kavanagh).

guard See –>garda.

gulpin Lout (from Irish *guilpín* /gul'p'i:n'/).

'I'm the two ends of a gulpin,' he said aloud to himself (Kavanagh).

'I've a houseful of gulpins who claim they don't know where the kettle is' (MacLaverty).

gurrier Good-for-nothing; a general term of contempt.

'That skinny little gurrier with him is just out of the gaol' (Plunkett).

'What's that gurrier saying about the country?' (J. O'Faolain).

hag 'Black hag' = cormorant (trans. of Irish –>*cailleach dhubh* /ka:l'əx ɣuv/).

'No one to keen him but the black hags that do be flying on the sea' (Synge).

An acropolis of cormorants, an extinct / Volcano where spiders spin, a purgatory / Guarded by hags and bristled with breakers (R. Murphy).

haggard Stackyard (cf. ON *heygarðr*).

Come to my haggard gate, my very doorstep (Campbell).

He had a sack of oats hidden in the old hay in the open shed in the haggard (Kavanagh).

haimes 'To make a haimes of' = to bungle, make a mess of (etym. unknown).

I started to puke ... I made a right haimes of my suit (F. O'Brien).

'He can mix up a [fishing] line and make a greater haimes of it than anyone I know' (Macken).

> *It is almost impossible for sensitive, intelligent, over-imaginative people not to make a hames of their development* (Cronin).

half (said about time) Half past.

> *There were nine minutes before half-eleven and we were going to the half-twelve mass* (Doyle).

> *Minogue could be in the city by one, his dinner eaten by half one ... ready for business by two* (Brady).

half-mounted A 'half-mounted gentleman' is a would-be gentleman. Also called a –>'half-sir'.

> *A Mr. Frank Skelton, one of the half-mounted gentlemen described in the early part of this work – a boisterous, joking, fat, young fellow* (Barrington).

half-sir Would-be gentleman.

> *'The near-gentry, these latter being termed locally 'half-sirs' or –>'half-mounted gentlemen'* (Flanagan).

handball Game played by hitting a ball called a 'handball' against a single wall, or three or four walls forming an alley; popular in Ireland esp. in last quarter of 19th century. See –>GAA and –>ball alley.

> *Cranly took a small grey handball from his pocket* (Joyce).

> *Handball of sorts was played against the back of Jimmy Shivnan's forge* (McGahern).

> *It was a fine evening and they were walking on the cement path past the hand-ball alley and the river was calm like soft glass* (Tóibín).

harvestman Casual farm labourer hired for the harvest.

> *We talked to a man who had been in America, and before that had often gone to England as a harvestman* (Synge).

hazard Cab-stand.

Mr Bloom went round the corner and passed the drooping nags of the hazard (Joyce).

hedge school Properly, a school held 'by the hedge-side', but in fact not always in the open air. These schools flourished in 18th century Ireland, providing education for Catholics, who were prevented by –>Penal laws from receiving formal schooling.

The first hedge-school I have seen: a crowd of half-savage looking lads and girls looked up from their studies in the ditch, their college or lecture-room being in a mud cabin hard by (Thackeray).

The young priest and his Latin would succeed in throwing the hedge schoolmaster and his problems completely into the shade (Carleton).

The hedge-school is held in a disused barn or hay-shed or byre (Friel).

heel The end or bottom part of something. 'In (On) the heel(s) of the hunt' = at the end, finally.

They rose suddenly and left me, to walk ... down to the village now that it was so fine in the heel of the day (S. O'Faolain).

Gunmen who drift in and then away, and the good-hearted young fellows who in the heel of the hunt lie stretched upon the hard earth, blood staining the snow (Flanagan).

On the heels of the hunt ... it is time we got away from this north/south bracketting on the creative and editorial level (Dawe).

herself The mistress of the house, the woman in question, 'your/my wife' (trans. of Irish *í féin* /iː feːn'/). Similarly –>himself.

'Where's herself, Jack Smith?' – 'She was delayed with her washing' (Lady Gregory).

The dinner was ghastly altogether with herself tight as usual (Iremonger trans.).

High Cross See –>Celtic Cross.

himself The master of the house, the man in question, 'your/my husband' (trans. of Irish *é féin* /eː f'eːn'/). Similarly –>herself.

'Himself's mother can speak it [i.e. Irish]' (G. Moore).

'Is himself inside?' (M. Kelly).

hokey Meaningless exclamation or mild expletive; also 'hokies'.

'Oh, be [= by] the hokey, the sammin [= salmon]'s broke in two!' (Shaw).

'By the hokies, there was a man in this place one time by the name of Ned Sullivan' ... That is how, even in my own lifetime, stories began (O'Connor).

hokies See preceding entry.

hooker Fishing smack (from Dutch *hoeker*).

A hooker whose destination was some fishing harbour in the Atlantic (G. Moore).

In the hooker –>itself it is not easy to get them [i.e. ponies] safely on their feet in the small space that is available (Synge).

hooley A wild party (etym. unknown).

'Up there on that mountain they had a feast and a hooley that went on for a year' (Kiely).

A lazy local hero who ... never missed a dance or a hooley or any other kind of mischief (Montague).

Two young men ... were coming home in the early hours of the morning from an all-night hooley well-stacked with whiskey and porter (Brown).

hoor = whore; a mild term of abuse, used about both men and women.

'That Phelan girl is a proper hoor,' my father says at table (Higgins).

'The captain is a hoor for social distinction' (Kiely).

'Get out of my corn, you hoors you' (Friel).

hosting The marshalling of armed forces.

The Hosting of the –>Sidhe (Title, Yeats).

Those long Sunday rambles in the mountains where once there had been a great hosting (Flanagan).

house The 'man of the house' is the master of a household (trans. of Irish *fear an tí* /f'ar ə(n) t'i:/). Similarly, the mistress is called the 'woman of the house' (*bean* /b'an/ *an tí*).

Early this morning the man of the house came over for me in a four-oared curagh [–>currach] (Synge).

The woman of the house told me to come along any time I liked (Iremonger trans.).

hullagone See –>ullagone.

hunker 'On one's hunkers' = in a squatting position, with the haunches, knees and ankles acutely bent; to 'hunker' is to assume this position (etym. unknown).

The dean rested back on his hunkers (Joyce).

–>Sheela na Gig / We look up at her / hunkered into her angle / under the eaves (Heaney).

[The car] passes John-Joe hunkered at the end of his –>loaning (Devlin).

hurley   Curved stick used in –>hurling; also called a –>caman.

Hurleys were dangerous weapons (O'Casey).

I killed a rat with my hurley (Doyle).

hurling   Irish ball-game similar to hockey, played with a stick called a –>caman or –>hurley; foremost among the sports played by the heroes of Ancient Ireland. See also –>camogie and –>GAA.

The librarian ... was also the hurling critic for the <u>Cork Examiner</u> (M. Keane).

'It was Croke Park for a hurling match, on Sunday, rain, hail, or snow' (E. O'Brien).

iijit   See –>eejit.

inch   Low meadow ground near a river (from Irish *inis* /in'əs'/ = island).

His poor bedraggled wife they would see driving the cows of a night time to the inches (Corkery).

'There was a –>banshee heard calling over the inches last night' (J. B. Keane).

Indian corn   Maize. Also 'Indian meal'.

Lord John Russell ... took measures for supplying the country with Indian corn (Trollope).

Indian-meal porridge and brown –>soda-bread, / Boiled eggs and buttermilk (R. Murphy).

Indian meal   See preceding entry.

GLOSSARY

in it   There, in existence; sometimes = alive (trans. of Irish *ann* /aun/).

'He was the grandest horse in the four –>baronies. He was forty-two years of age when he died, and they –>waked him same as ye'd wake a Christian. They had whisky and porther – and bread – and a –>piper in it' (Somerville and Ross).

'We wouldn't see him want anything while he was in it' (Joyce).
'It's the times that are in it ... The people haven't the money' (Trevor).

intirely   See –>entirely.

Invincibles   Extremist secret society in the late 19th century.

The fellow that turned queen's evidence on the invicibles (Joyce).

Lord Cavendish and Mr. Burke, both British government officials, were killed in 1882 by the 'Invincibles'. The Invincibles were an extreme wing of the –>Fenians (Behan).

IRA   The Irish Republican Army, which became the Army of the Irish Republic in 1919. It split in 1921 into the 'Old IRA' consisting of those who accepted the –>Treaty, and the 'New IRA' or the –>Irregulars, who opposed it. Since then split into a 'Provisional' and an 'Official' IRA.

Her son Paddins was a sort of Neo-Old I.R.A man and dressed for the part. He wore a cap, a sports coat with leather buttons and split up the middle and knee breeches (Behan).

The Northern Ireland Secretary ... has repeated his statement that –>Sinn Fein and the IRA could be brought into the political process (Irish Times).

Irish Free State   In the English language, the name of the –>Twenty-six

Counties that were established as a separate state in 1922; in Irish: –>*Saorstát Éireann.* The name was changed in 1937 to –>*Éire,* or in the English language, *Ireland.*

Crippen was in his day a sergeant-major in the Free State Army and played –>*Gaelic football* (Behan).

Irish mile   The Irish mile (still in rustic use) is 2.240 yards, the English mile being 1.760 yards.

Ballyhaunis was only eight miles from Kelly's Court; though they were Irish miles, it is true (Trollope).
The city of Limerick and the eye specialist were twenty Irish miles away (E. O'Brien).

Irishry   The native Irish.

Cast your mind on other days / That we in coming days may be / Still the indomitable Irishry (Yeats).

That chance meeting ... / conscribed me of the Irishry forever (Hewitt).

Irregulars   Members of the –>IRA who rejected the –>Treaty.

On this occasion he was an Irregular guerilla ... seated high up on a lorry (S. O'Faolain).

An affable Irregular, / A heavily-built Falstaffian man, / Comes cracking jokes of civil war (Yeats).

itinerant   See –>traveller and –>tinker.

itself   Commonly used for emphasis, = just, even (cf. Irish *féin* /fe:n'/ = -self, even).

'What'd I care if you brought me a drift of chosen females,' standing in their –>*shifts itself'* (Synge).

'They may not be ... my own words. But if they're not itself I know what they mean' (Kilroy).

GLOSSARY

Ivy Day October 6th, so called from the ivy leaf worn as a symbol of mourning for the political leader Charles Stewart Parnell, who died on that day in 1891; ivy is associated with his estate in County Wicklow.

Ivy Day in the Committee Room (Title, Joyce).

jackeen Dubliner (from the English name Jack + Irish dimin.).

He was only a Dublin jackeen (Joyce).

There's a little jackeen from Dublin working here and he'd make you feel rightly ashamed (Iremonger trans.).

jar A drink; 'jarred' = intoxicated.

Old fellows, a bit jarred and singing, and fellows –>leaving their –>mots home to Drumcondra after the pictures (Behan).

'I'm not jarred, Pop ... just a few jars, that's all' (Brown).

jarvey Driver, esp. of a –>side car.

The jarvey was asked why he didn't take me to Lower Mount Street (G. Moore).

The jarvey, who was waiting for him, bowed as he received the bags from the manservant (S. O'Faolain).

jaunting car = –>side car.

jennet Usually = hinney, the offspring of a she-ass and a stallion.

A lady known to her acquaintances as the Jennet, a title which she could not, because of one unwanted child, honestly claim (Kiely).

I took a stick and beat the reluctant jennet into pulling the load uphill (McGahern).

jig Quick, lively dance.

82

The fiddler sawed his merriest jigs (Barrington).

Jigs were danced on the kitchen table with more solemn fervour than after a cricket match (Bowen).

jintleman See –>gentleman.

jobber Small tradesman, cattle dealer.

'If I am not mistaken ... you are Tom Burke the cattle-dealer.' 'Tom Burke the jobber ... No mistake about it' (Kickham).

Dublin made me and no little town / With the country closing in on its streets / The cattle walking proudly on its pavements/ The jobbers, the –>gombeenmen and the cheats / Devouring the fair-day between them (D. MacDonagh).

'I think you have the nerve of a Limerick cattle jobber' (Flanagan).

kale-kanon See –>colcannon.

keen The ritual wailing over a corpse (from Irish *caoin* /ki:n'/). Also verb.

'Am I left here to keen him alone?' (Lady Gregory).
When the coffin was in the grave ... the keen broke out again more passionately than before (Synge).

[The gull's cry] was everywhere around me, a disembodied keening in the calm, white air (Banville).

keep The central tower of a mediaeval castle.

This is the country of the Norman tower, / The graceless keep, the bleak and slitted eye (D. MacDonagh).

Now we move among ruins, –>peasants gawking at the broken, roofless keeps of Munster and Connaught (Flanagan).

keeping To be 'on one's keeping' is to be on the run, in hiding (from 'keep' in the sense 'board and lodging').

Their father made them, now and then, a brief and stealthy visit ... he was, as the phrase is in Munster, 'on his keeping' (Le Fanu).

'He is on his keeping now in Iveragh, to avoid arrest' (Flanagan).

kelp Seaweed, burned and used as fertilizer (etym. unknown).

The people have taken advantage of this dry moment to begin the burning of kelp, and all the islands are lying in a volume of grey smoke (Synge).

The discovery of a chemical substitute for iodine ... affected kelp production (Irish Times).

kerne Light-armed Irish foot-soldier (from Irish *ceithearnach* /kˈehərnəx/).

'I have seen hanging enough in merry England, and care not to see the gibbets of Irish kernes' (Thackeray).

A wood-kerne / Escaped from the massacre (Heaney).

kesh Pathway; drain made to leave passage for water in wet ground (from Irish *cosán* /kosaːn/ = path, passage). 'Kesh' may also be an alternative spelling of –>'kish', basket.

A kesh could mean a track some call a <u>causey</u> / Raised above the wetness of the bog, / Or the causey where it bridged old streams and drains. / It steadies me to tell these things. Also / I cannot mention keshes or the ford / Without my father's shade appearing to me (Heaney).

The haylifter drawn by Nellie, our huge Clydesdale mare ... rumbles across the wide ditches called keshes that moat and drain the meadows, bridged by heavy sleeper logs (Devlin).

kilt Exhausted (= 'killed').

'I must be going,' he replied. 'I ought to be on the road an hour ago.' 'You'll be kilt,' returned Nellie ... 'wudout [= without] gettin' a wink uv [= of] sleep' (Kickham).

'The old fellow kept us at our rosaries for a solid hour. My knees are kilt' (Flanagan).

Kiltartan English with an exaggeratedly Irish sentence structure, as used by Lady Gregory in her popular writings (from the name of a district near her home, Coole Park in County Galway). See section on The Two Languages in Ireland.

As they greeted each other, Denzil recognised the purest Kiltartan on their lips (Longford).

King's County Former name for County Offaly (so called in honour of King Philip of Spain, husband of Mary I of England, during whose reign the county was colonised). See also –>Queen's County.

[He] had been away in a situation for many years as a coach-man in the King's County (G. Moore).

kip Lodging(-house), brothel (cf. Danish *kippe*). Dublin's notorious red-light district was known as 'the kips'.

'We used to emigrate to get work ... I slept in every kip in Scotland' (Kiely).

A very interesting way of getting a kip for the weekend (Behan).

kippeen Twig, little stick (from Irish *cipín* /k'ip'i:n'/).

A sod of –>turf stuck on a –>sally switch or kippeen, and placed in the thatch of an Irish –>cabin, is the sign of 'good liquor within' (W. Wilde).

'A niggard with her eyes on kippeens, that would skin a flea for its hide' (Yeats).

kish Wicker basket (from Irish *cis* /k'is'/ = basket; of Scandinavian origin, cf. ON *kass*); may also be spelt –>'kesh'.

A train of his companions leading their cars [= carts] loaded with kishes of turf (Edgeworth).

The kish ... served to wash, strain, and 'dish' the potatoes, feed the pig, or rock the child, as occasion might require (Hall).

kitchen Any kind of food eaten with bread, etc. as a relish.

In the winter when the milk was scarce they ate the potatoes with a kitchen made of salt and water, or with a herring, or even a pinch of a herring (Corkery).

knowe Nut (from Irish *cnó* /kno:/). 'The Maid of the Sweet Browne Knowe' is a well-known song.

A young man /... Who has lately come a-courting / The maid of the Sweet Brown Knowe (Song).

Lambeg Large drum used by marching bands associated with the –>Orange Order, so called after a district in County Antrim.

Everybody wears an –>Orange sash and you can see the sweat pouring off them as they wallop away at the drums. These are special large drums known as 'Lambegs' and the drummer uses canes to beat them with (Behan).

'The rattle of the bin-lid had challenged the supremacy of the Lambeg drum' (Reid).

A Lambeg drum is the focus at an –>Orange rally (Irish Times).

Land League Organisation founded 1879, aiming at abolishing landlordism.

'The difficulty the Government find themselves in is that the Land League is apparently a legal organisation,' said Lord Dungory (G. Moore).

Pay no rent and keep the harvest, this I am sure is Land League law, / And if the landlord asks you for it give to him an oaten straw (Song).

lashings An abundance, plenty.

All washed down with lashings of strong tea (Behan).

Suddenly everywhere we look we are being served lashings of magic (Irish Times).

lawn Expanse of grass, often unmown.
Among a rich man's flowering lawns (Yeats).

In Ireland a 'lawn' does not mean turf subjected to fine mowing; it means that grass expanse that in England is called a park (Bowen).

The horses when they were let loose wandered back to the lawn, searching out the sweet grass (Banville).

lazy bed Spade ridges for potatoes; the sod under the ridge is not dug, but the bed is built up on top of the grass with sods and soil dug from the trenches between the ridges.

–>Peasants were forever sub-dividing their tiny holdings so that a son might marry, build his –>cabin, dig his lazybed of potatoes (Flanagan).

The one drawback was its heavy labour input, but the lazy bed was still three times as productive as horse-plough cultivation in England and France at the time (Irish Times).

leannansidhe See –>linnaun shee.

leave Accompany, 'take'.

I eased him gently into the passenger's seat and started the engine. 'Leave us home,' Plunkett said (Bolger).

One night ... he leaves her home from a dance (Kiely).

GLOSSARY

lep = leap.

'[They] came over the river lepping the stones' (Synge).

The lobster was ready after all, the man handed it over ... 'Lepping fresh, sir,' said the man, 'fresh in this morning' (Beckett).

leprechaun A pigmy sprite in Irish folk-lore, a fairy cobbler (from Irish *leipreachán* /lˈepˈrˈəxaːn/).

He romanticized Ireland's heroic past, which he peopled ... with ghosts and fairies and leprechauns (Murdoch).

I ... become, not a poet of the heart, / but a leipreachan at his last, / making unwearable golden shoes (Hartnett).

likely Promising.

[Nelly said] 'There'll be some likely lads there [at the wedding] to'night, an' who knows what luck I might have' (Kickham).

'You've turned me a likely –>gaffer in the end of all' (Synge).

linnaun shee Fairy mistress (from Irish *leanann sidhe* /lˈanaːn sˈiː/).

Like a love-sick leanannsidhe, / She has my heart in thrall (Song).

'Glory be to God, women, it's a fairy woman – the Linnaun Shee herself – has got my Jamesie!' (Fitzmaurice).

liss Ring-fort (from Irish *lios* /lˈis/).

'Lisses and forts shall be at your command' (Song).

The bush-grown 'liss', that ... records the labours of a bygone race (Le Fanu).

loaning = lane; also an open piece of land where cows are milked.

GLOSSARY

As I went down the loaning / the wind shifting in the hedge was like / an old one's [–>ould] whistling speech (Heaney).

I am no longer afraid of –>banshees and black dogs and the living dead, and I look up the loanings to the houses where the neighbours congregated for the evening's –>crack (Devlin).

lough = lake (from Irish *loch* /lox/).

Our lights looked over the lough to the lights of Bangor (MacNeice).

Right along the lough shore / A smoke of flies / Drifts thick in the sunset (Heaney).

loy Long narrow one-eared spade (from Irish *láí* /laːiː/).

'It was with a loy the like of that I killed my father' (Synge).

He took up billhook and loy / To win the ground he would never own (Muldoon).

lug Ear (perhaps from Scandinavian).

'Are you hurt?' 'I've a crack over the lug, an' a scratch across the small o' me back' (Boucicault).

Cowley's red lugs and Adam's apple in the door of the sheriff's office (Joyce).

A performance which merited a belt of one [i.e. a bottle] across the lug (Irish Times).

Lughnasa /luːnəsə/ The festival of Lugh /luː/, the old Celtic God of the Harvest.

Dancing at Lughnasa (Title, Friel).

machree Term of endearment, 'my dear' (from Irish poss. pron. + mutated form (/xriː/) of *croí* /kriː/ = heart).

'Don't be startin' them fashions now, Mary Machree, / Where the Mountains of Mourne sweep down to the sea' (French).

'Ben Machree,' said Mr Dedalus, clapping Ben's fat shoulder-blade (Joyce).

madder   See –>medher.

Martello tower   Squat circular tower of a type built round the coast of Ireland during the threat of Napoleonic invasion (from Mortella, a tower in Corsica on which the Irish Martello towers are modelled).

You can see the white Martello-tower-like houses of the landlords (G. Moore).

Cycling from Dublin city towards the Wicklow hills, he and a friend stopped to call on three young men who lived in a Martello tower (Kiely).

mass cave   Cave in which mass was said in –>Penal times. See also next entry.

The militia tramped the hills searching for Mass caves (Flanagan).

mass rock   Rock at which mass was said in –>Penal times. See also preceding entry.

I explored the mountain, roving farther and farther with my dogs, to the mass rock at Altamuskin (Montague).

matchmaker   Formerly, one who professionally arranged matches, usually on the basis of economic considerations.

Mary Murray, the Irish Match-Maker (Title, Carleton).

'After the famine times, when the runaway matches gave over [= stopped], and the match-making come in' (Molloy).

Dan Paddy Andy O'Sullivan was the last matchmaker to operate in Kerry. From his modest home ... he was responsible for directing four hundred couples to the altar of God (J. B. Keane).

ma'vourneen Term of endearment; lit. 'my sweetheart' (from Irish poss. pron. + mutated form (/vu:rn'i:n'/) of *muirnín* /mu:rn'i:n'/ = sweetheart).

'Brian, <u>mavourneen</u>, did you see him goin' anywhere?' (Carleton).

Come back to –>Erin, mavourneen, mavourneen (Song).

ma'vrone Alas; lit. 'my grief' (from Irish poss. pron. + mutated form (/vro:n/) of *brón* /bro:n/ = grief).

Where is my chief, my master, this bleak night, mavrone? / O, cold, cold, miserable cold is this bleak night for Hugh (Mangan, trans.).

'Mavrone, mavrone! the man has died' (Yeats).

medher Square wooden drinking cup (Irish *meadar* /m'adər/, English 'mether': a bowl for mead, OE *meodu*).

He is no better than a spawlpeen [–>spalpeen] ... When I was there last, we had nothing but a madder to drink out of (Swift).

The medher of dark strong foamy ale (Joyce).

medical hall Chemist's shop.

If there are eleven medical halls in the street there are <u>fourteen</u> establishments licensed for the sale of you-know-what ... no wonder the chemists' shops flourish (Robinson).

The medical hall where I was serving apprenticeship (E. O'Brien).

mich To play truant (apparently from OFr. *muchier* = hide, skulk).

With Leo Dillon and a boy named Mahoney I planned a day's miching (Joyce).

I mitch from school (Higgins).

Mick Used generically of any Irishman (= the Christian name Mick, from Michael).

'The Micks are hardly going to fall for a long-lost-relative-showing-up routine' (Brady).

'The only thing that really annoys me is if other builders don't bother to ask your name and immediately call me Mick or –>Paddy because I'm Irish' (Irish Times).

middleman One who takes farms on long leases and lets them again to under-tenants, at exorbitant rents.

The agent was one of your middlemen, who grind the face of the poor (Edgeworth).

The –>rack-rents ... were, of course, themselves the result of the Middleman system (Corkery).

Milesians In Irish mythology, the ancestors of the present inhabitants of Ireland.

Shannon ran red with Milesian blood (Drennan).

mind To remember.

'Do you mind Spats at the law classes?' (McGahern).

'I do mind it well,' Ellen said. 'Haven't you told it a hundred times till my head's turned listening to it' (Devlin).

Molly Maguires Members of an anti-landlord secret society which flourished in Ireland 1835-55 and spread to America. The members wore women's clothing.

A crowd of known Molly Maguires were coming over from Tipperary (Kilroy).

GLOSSARY

	The Molly Maguires stepped out of the trees on the drive, three stark men in tattered dresses, with cropped heads and murderous eyes, carrying shovels over their shoulders (Banville).
mot	Girl (a form of 'mort' = woman; perhaps from French).
	And I'd not like the Sabbath to bend / So I said I would wait until Monday / For my redheaded mot in Ringsend (Song).
	'When you're with your mot an' your kids' (Doyle).
musha	Well, indeed (from Irish *muise* /mis'ə/, from *má is ea, más ea* = if so, even so). Variant: wisha.
	But Larry not one word did say, / Nor changed till he came to 'King William', / Then, musha! his colour grew white (Song).
	'Muise, isn't a hundred welcomes enough for any man?' (Behan).
naggin	See –>noggin.
national school	Part of a nationwide school system offering elementary education, established 1831.
	Look at the National School: throughout the country it is commonly by the –>chapel side – it is a Catholic school (Thackeray).
	'I'm surprised at boys like you, educated, reading such stuff. I could understand it if you were ... National School boys' (Joyce).
	She was a national schoolteacher and a very proper woman (Friel).
night line	Fishing line with hooks for catching eels, laid out from a boat or on a beach.

I rowed as he let out the night line, his fingers baiting each twisted hook (McGahern).

'Nightlines,' I say, 'a practice common in the South of Ireland. Two metal rods with a line of hooks strung between them, to be jammed in the sand at low tide, the hooks skewered with rag or lug-worms ... then left to simmer as the ocean passes over them until morning' (Jordan).

Ninety-Eight The Insurrection of 1798.

Who fears to speak of Ninety-Eight? / Who blushes at the name? / When cowards mock the patriot's fate / Who hangs his head for shame? (T. Moore).

In ninety-eight, two military roads cut it [i.e. a plateau] across and across like a scissors (S. O'Faoláin).

noggin Quarter pint; also 'naggin' (Irish *naigín* /nag'i:n'/).

'I'm not the man now to be placed among the other riff-raff of the family over a basket of potatoes, wid [= with] a black clerical coat upon me, and a noggin of milk under my arm!' (Carleton).

It was a great dinner if they got a noggin of buttermilk from the cook (G. Moore).

A bent hag crossed from Cassidy's clutching a naggin bottle by the neck (Joyce).

nor Than (after comparatives).

'The housekeeper was an –>ould woman, with a pipe in her mouth, and not a tooth left, and better nor eighty years ould' (Le Fanu).

We said more nor our prayers in the slums of North Dublin where I was born (Behan).

'I was kept a bit longer nor I reckoned,' Peigin gasped (Lavin).

notionate	Obstinate, self-opinionated. *'Agnes was too notionate to work in a factory'* (Friel)
Ogham	/ɔgəm/oːm/ Ancient alphabet of twenty letters, each formed of strokes on either side of the angle of a stone or crossing it (from *Ogma*, name of legendary inventor). *The Ogham from her pillar-stone / In tract of time will wear away* (Ferguson). *The Ogham problem hardly has been discussed at all* (Irish Times).
o'hone	Alas (from Irish *ochón* /oxoːn/). *'I crying out, Ohone'* (Synge).
oinseach	Fool, usually a foolish woman (Irish *óinseach* /oːn's'əx/). *'An ill-bred band of amadáns [–>omadaun] an' oinseachs'* (T. Murphy).
'Oireachtas¹	/or'əxtəs/ The Irish Parliament, which has two Houses: the –>Dáil and the –>Seanad. *Oireachtas* is properly preceded by the definite article (which in Irish prefixes t- to certain nouns): *An tOireachtas*. *Business in the Houses of the Oireachtas continued more or less as usual* (Irish Times). *Only two members of the Cabinet ... have been members of the Oireachtas for as long as she has* (Irish Times).
'Oireachtas²	/or'əxtəs/ Festival, e.g. the annual cultural festival of the Irish language; properly *Oireachtas na Gaeilge* /nə geːl'g'ə/ = of Irish (Gaelic). *I'm told that he won some prize or other in the Oireachtas* (Iremonger trans.).
old one	See –>ould.

ologoan See –>ullagone.

ollav Man of learning, master poet (from Irish *ollamh* /oləv/).

To George Sigerson / Patriot and Sage, Bard of the –>Gael and –>Gall, / Teacher and Healer, Ollamh of subtle lore (Dedication, T. MacDonagh).

A generous following of ollavs and bards with their law-books and their verse-scrolls (F. O'Brien).

omadhaun Fool (from Irish *amadán* /amǝda:n/).

'Why, ye omadhaun', says he, 'you won't see home for six months' (Boucicault).

'They get these thundering big country fellows, omadhauns, you know, to drill' (Joyce).

Like an omadhaun in a love poem (Kiely).

one 'the one' = 'the same'.

'I can't keep my mind on everything at the one time' (M. Keane).

I said it is all the one evil Catholic or Protestant which greatly scandalised him (Kilroy).

Orange Applied to the ultra-Protestant party, in reference to the society of Orangemen founded in 1795. The name probably referred to William of Orange.

Oh! the French are in the bay, / They'll be here by break of day, / And the Orange will decay, / Says the –>Shan Van Vocht (Song).

In bowler hats and Sunday suits / Orange sashes, polished boots (R. Murphy).

The Orange bands banged past in the summer (Montague).

ould	= old; often spelt 'ould' or 'auld', reflecting a pronunciation approaching [auld] rather than [ould]. 'Old/ould ones' are most often old women. See also –>wan.

'The ould man was in bed' (Kickham).

'He bought a book from an old one in Liffey street for two bob' (Joyce).

'The oul' ones'll be talking, an' once they start you don't know how it'll end' (O'Casey). |
| **ouns** | = wounds (of Christ).

'Tare [–>tear] an' ouns!' roared Murphy, 'how Andy runs!' (Lover).

'For this, O dearly beloved, is the genuine Christine: body and soul and blood and ouns' (Joyce). |
| **outside car** | = –>side car. |
| **outsider** | = –>side car. |
| **oxter** | The under-side of the upper arm; the armpit (from OE *óxta*).

'If poetry as well as music could be squeezed out of an Irish bagpipes, I'd say that ballad came out of that bag under his oxter' (Kickham).

He'd a jam roll under his oxter (Behan).
'Ah, Sweet Jaysus [= Jesus].' Her voice soared. 'She's in –>glaur to the oxters on me nice clean floor' (Devlin). |
| **Paddy** | Used generically of any Irishman (from the Christian name Patrick).

The Paddies over here are very much against that sort of thing - that anyone should pretend in front of the English that things are not too good in Ireland (Iremonger trans). |

They called everyone Paddy and told dirty stories (E. O'Brien).

He complained about his workmates' 'thick Paddy' jokes (Irish Times).

Pale   'The Pale' was the area around Dublin dominated early by English influence and under English jurisdiction.

Into the very heart of the Pale, into Dublin itself, this –>Gaelic-speaking Ireland flowed in many streams (Corkery).

What of the O'Tooles and the O'Byrnes who ... raided from the hills, snapping at the edges of the English Pale? (Brady).

pampootie   Shoe of untanned hide (from Irish *pampúta* /pampu:tə/).

It was decided to make me a pair of pampooties, which I have been wearing to-day among the rocks. They consist simply of a piece of raw cowskin, with the hair outside, laced over the toe and round the heel with two ends of fishing-line that work round and are tied above the instep (Synge).

'Oh be my lady,' he sings, 'and in Limerick laces your delicate ways shall airily pass, with quiet feet in your blue pampooties and guinea hens on the daisied grass' (Kiely).

pandy   Dish of mashed potatoes.

She was engaged in making a 'pandy', with a view to breakfast (Kickham).

You were given pandy. The butter was yellow and floating in a crevice on the top and you swallowed the stuff down without chewing (E. O'Brien).

pandybat   Leaded leather strap (cf. 'pandy' = a stroke from a cane or strap on the hand as punishment; allegedly from Latin *pande palmam* or *manum*, 'hold out your hand').

The echoing corridors resounded with the noise of the pandy-bat (Higgins).

Fleming held out his hand. The pandybat came down on it with a loud smacking sound (Joyce).

parlatic = 'paralytic' with drink.

'Young blades getting parlatic on the smell of a cork (Plunkett).
She'd been really drunk, absolutely paralytic (Doyle).

Partition The division of Ireland into Northern Ireland and the –>Irish Free State or –> *Saorstát Éireann*.

This vast [17th century] –>Plantation is the origin of Ireland's modern Partition problem (S. O'Faolain).

pattern A gathering at a holy site in honour of the patron saint ('pattern' = 'patron').

Such a pattern! – such a sight of tents had never been seen by the oldest man in the parish (Hall).

The old man told me in Irish that they had been at a pattern – a sort of semi-religious festival like the well-known festivals of Brittany (Synge).

peasant The common word for country people who are not landowners.

I caught a glimpse of the ragged peasantry following the hunt (G. Moore).

The poor peasant talking to himself in the stable door — / An ignorant peasant deep in dung (Kavanagh).

The romantic notion that we Irish have of making one leap from the peasant's –>cabin to the good job in the Civil Service (Daly).

peel Young salmon (etym. unknown).

> *When the peel were running they fished at the turn of the tide* (M. Kelly).

> *'I've a peal salmon that I've boiled all in a piece'* (MacMahon).

peeler Formerly the common name for a policeman in Ireland; from Sir Robert Peel, who in 1814 instituted the paramilitary force that became the Royal Irish Constabulary, the –>RIC.

> *'They're taking me to the peelers to have me hanged for slaying you'* (Synge)

> *With a banging of boots and a clatter of buckles two peelers came running* (Banville).

Penal Referring to Penal Laws passed against Catholics in the 17th and 18th centuries.

> *Hennessys had lost wealth and place but by no means good repute when they scorned to take the Protestant Communion in the Penal Days* (K. O'Brien).

> *Penal Laws had robbed the MacOwens of their wide acres* (Flanagan).

> *'An old crucifix belonging to the penal days'* (Kiely).

pike Long slender shaft with an iron or steel head; the traditional weapon of Irish rebellion.

> *Though lads are making pikes again / For some conspiracy* (Yeats).

> *There were also a number of old –>Fenian pikes, a weapon much favoured by Eamon de Valera* (Murdoch).

pioneer One who belongs to a temperance society founded in the 19th century. The Pioneer badge is a white enamel plaque with a burning heart, the symbol of the passion of Jesus.

> *'God sent Father Cullen, the great Jesuit, to found the pioneer league of total abstinence'* (Kiely).

'My father's a pioneer' (J. Johnston).

Three were on Guinness. The fourth wore a pioneer pin – badge of total abstinence (J. O'Faolain).

piper   One who plays the –>*uilleann* /il'ən/ pipes.

'Here's the –>hooker being rowed into the bay bringing the piper and story-tellers from Aran' (G. Moore).

A piper ... playing his pipes and drinking –>poteen and the people dancing round him (Synge).

pishogue   Superstition, witchcraft (from Irish *piseog* /p'is'o:g/). Also 'pish(e)rogue'.

'Pishrogue and nonsense,' said Hughie (Kiely).

The sower ... must throw some turf over the rump of each horse. There were a hundred pishogues like those ones, and the harvest depended on them (Flanagan).

pishrogue   See preceding entry.

Plantation   Colonisation, esp. that of Ulster in the 17th century. See also next entry.

'What exactly are you working on?' Eileen asked ... 'Oh, the Williamite plantations ... it's real research anyway' (White).

The parish in which I was brought up lies in Tyrone ... it escaped resettling at the time of the Plantation (Montague).

planter   Usually an English or Scottish settler 'planted' on forfeited land in the 17th century. See preceding entry.

The culture common to both –>Gaelic and Planter houses compares favourably with that of families of equal rank in England (Corkery).

'They have their hagiology – brave English planters defending their homes' (Flanagan).

planxty	In Irish music: a lively harp tune (etym. unknown). *The –>pipers jerked from their bags appropriate planxties to every jolly sentiment* (Barrington). *Playing his own planxties and reels* (Corkery).
poirse	= porch; also passage or laneway. *A farmer using the poirse of a neighbour as a short cut for his turf or corn* (Corkery).
polthogue	Blow, punch (from Irish *paltóg* /palto:g/). *'I'd have liked to see your face when you got that polthogue in the –>gob'* (Boucicault).
pooka	Goblin, sometimes appearing in the form of a horse, bull et al. (from Irish *púca* /pu:kə/). *It is a popular belief – kept up probably to prevent children eating them when over ripe – that the pooka, as he rides over the country, defiles the blackberries at Michaelmas and Holly-eve* (W. Wilde). *He had all the traditional stuff – the –>pisherogues about the fairies and the pooka* (O'Connor).
pookawn	See –>pucaun.
poor mouth	Facial expression of misery (trans. of Irish *béal bocht* /b'e:l boxt/). *'They were always making what we call 'the poor mouth' – a mendicant habit of centuries, I suppose'* (S. O'Faolain). *'We don't go about cryin' poverty and puttin' a poor mouth on ourselves the way they do'* (Reid).
poor scholar	Wandering student; one who frequented –>hedge schools. *The Poor Scholar* (Title, Carleton).

The 'poor scholars' caused him but little surprise, for these were now an old institution in the place (Corkery).

Race memories of →hedge schools and the poor scholar were stirred, as boys, like uncertain flocks of birds on bicycles, came long distances from the villages and outlying farms to grapple with calculus and George Gordon and the delta of the River Plate (McGahern).

poteen   Illicit whiskey (from Irish *poitín* /pot'i:n'/, lit. 'little pot').

'And she with a stale stink of poteen on her from selling in the shop' (Synge).

In those days the police minded their own business, like murder, robbery, rebellion and poteen (Kiely).

'I think youre not accustomed to potcheen punch in the evening after your tea' (Shaw).

power   A large number. The phrase 'more power to' expresses approbation, = 'good for!'

Archbishop Whateley, more power to him! would back us at a →hurling (W. Wilde).

'Eighty jugs. Six cups and a broken one. Two plates. A power of glasses' (Synge).

'There's a bad time out there lately, with a power of banks failing' (Molloy).

PP   = parish priest.

The Reverend Mr. Lutterell, curate to the suspended P.P. (Kilroy).

'Changes were made when the p.p. got a whiff of it' (Trevor).

praties   = potatoes.

'Them's purty [= pretty] pratees, Mrs. Rooney' (Lover).

Oh the praties they are small over here (Song).

prechan Crow, rook; nonsensical chatterer (from Irish *préachán* /p'r'e:xa:n/).

It was a little <u>prechan</u> not five years old (Croker).

Prod = Protestant.

The new cemetry is segregated. Prods to the right, –>Fenians to the left' (Reid).

province One of the four historical divisions of Ireland: Ulster, Munster, Leinster, Connacht /kɔnəxt/.

For months he tramped the roads of the four provinces (Flanagan).

pucaun Open boat, fishing smack (from Irish *púcán* /pu:ka:n/). Also 'pookawn' et al.

Two or three pookawns – lateen-rigged boats, said to be of Spanish origin (Synge).

The man leaned out of the pucaun boat beside him (Macken).

quare = queer; sometimes used as an intensifier. The spelling 'quare' reflects a common Hiberno-English pronunciation.

She had given them all a quare fright, she told him (McLaverty).

The Quare Fellow (Title, Behan).

'It could be a quare good match for our Beth' (Reid).

Queen's County Former name for County Laois /li:s'/ (so called after Mary I of England, during whose reign the county was colonised). See also –>King's County.

One [i.e. Bowen] went to Ireland, to Queens County ... one settled in Devonshire, one again went to Ireland, to County Cork — and he was my ancestor (Bowen).

When this became known in the Queen's County ... the hospitality of the –>Anglo-Irish landlords was extended to him (Lewis).

rackrent Excessive rent, usually of a farm; to 'rack' meant to charge excessive rent.

The Landlordes theare vse most shamefullie to racke theire Tenantes (Spenser).

Castle Rackrent (Title, Edgeworth).

Many others are not true landlords at all, but –>middlemen to whom the land has been let for reletting, and many of these employ the barbarous practice of the 'rack rent' (Flanagan).

raking A 'raking pot of tea' was originally enjoyed in secret by ladies after a late-night party, and was the occasion of much gossip and comment on the departed guests (cf. Danish *rivegilde*).

And then dances and balls, and the ladies all finishing with a raking pot of tea in the morning (Edgeworth).

A dance, as usual, wound up the entertainment, and what was then termed a 'raking pot of tea' put a finishing stroke, in jollity and good humour, to such a revel as I never saw before (Barrington).

rampar Enclosure, 'rampart'.

The hay is being cut over in John's Johnny's rampar and the sound of the tractor comes lurching over the low hedges (Devlin).

rann Verse (from Irish *rann* /ran/).

Know, that I would accounted be / True brother of a company / That sang, to sweeten Ireland's wrong, / Ballad and story, rann and song (Yeats).

The ranns of ancient Celtic bards (Joyce).

GLOSSARY

rapparee   Irish pikeman (–>pike) or irregular soldier, of the kind prominent during the war of 1688-92; an Irish bandit, robber, or free-booter (from Irish *rapaire* /rapər'ə/ = short pike).

Dark night with no moon to guard / Roads from the rapparees (R. Murphy).

Sarsfield stole out of Limerick City one night with Galloping Hogan, a brave rapparee (E. O'Brien).

rasher   Commonly used for 'rasher of bacon'.

They had rashers and eggs with black pudding and white pudding and a Cork –>drisheen (Behan).

In the window of Foley's the elderly assistant was laying out rows of rashers (Trevor).

rath   /ra:þ/raþ/ Ring-fort (from Irish *ráth* /ra:/).

The rath which he revered has been, to our knowledge, ploughed up (W. Wilde).

In these raths the defeated may have lived (Dunsany).

RDS   = Royal Dublin Society. The RDS plays an important part in Art and Science, Industry and Agriculture, and hosts an annual Horse Show.

It's Dublin Horse Show time once again which means that when not competing in the RDS, visitors and Dubliners alike will be racing around a taxing course of social gatherings (Irish Times).

RC   = Roman Catholic.

Resp girl (R.C.) wishes to hear of post in fruit or pork shop (Joyce).

'I hear your sister's chummed up with Dennehy,' Matilda said ... 'RC of course?' (Trevor).

redshank	Red-legged; a bare-legged person. Used of the Celtic inhabitants of Ireland and the Scottish Highlands; sometimes apparently = the ancient people of the Picts.

[Robert the Bruce] sente ouer his ... brother Edwarde with a power of Skottes and Redshankes into Irelande (Spenser).

The rude, red-shanked figures that clustered about the trees (Thackeray).

'Scotsmen, red-shank Highlanders' (Flanagan).

relief works	Public works undertaken for the relief of unemployment. See also –>famine road.

Nearly every foot of it [i.e. the road] ... has been built up in different years of famine by the people in the neighbourhood working on government relief works (Synge).

renege	/ri I ni:g/ To go back on one's word (from Latin *renegare*).

'I swear to God I'll wed him, and I'll not renege' (Synge).

'We fought for the royal Stuarts that reneged us against the Williamites and they betrayed us' (Joyce).

He found it easy in most cases to renege on oral agreements (Irish Times).

Republican	One who opposed the Treaty with England in 1921 – unlike the –>Free Staters, who accepted the status of Free State for Ireland. See –>Civil War.

'If you're a Republican they make you sing "God save the King", an' if you're loyal they'll make you sing the –>"Soldiers' Song"' (O'Casey).

On a roof-top near O'Connell Bridge a Republican sniper lay watching (O'Flaherty).

Resident Magistrate	See –>RM.

Ribbonmen Local groups which were part of an underground of agrarian secret societies, 'Ribbon Societies'. Members were known as Ribbonmen in the 19th century as they had been known as –>Whiteboys in the 18th century.

Confessions of a Reformed Ribbonman (Title, Carleton).
The master was for hunting the Ribbonmen: / A secret band, swearing oaths by moonlight, / Refusing to pay tithes or rent to the landlord, / Who battered on lonely doors after midnight, / And wore round their sleeves a white band (R. Murphy).

A distant kinsman ... had been stabbed to death by a scarecrow band of Ribbonsmen (Kilroy).

RIC = Royal Irish Constabulary (disbanded 1921).

One of those unequalled judges of the moral temperature of a crowd, a sergeant of the R.I.C. (Somerville and Ross). *Another R.I.C. barracks had been attacked and stripped of arms* (Farrell).

Rising The Easter Rising of 1916.

'When the Rising took place he acted like a true Irish hero' (Behan).

RM = Resident Magistrate; formerly, a stipendiary magistrate in Ireland.

Some Experiences of an Irish R.M. (Title, Somerville and Ross).

Charges of assault were prepared for the R.M. (Farrell).

round tower Tall, slender tower belonging to a monastic settlement. A popular symbol of Ireland's past.

We turned inland, past the Round Tower and the roofless church (M. Keane).

Let the round tower stand aloof / In a world of bursting mortar (MacNeice).

RTE = Raidió Telefís Éireann /rad'i:o: t'el'əf'i:s' e:r'ən/, the Irish sound and television broadcasting corporation.

After I had appeared on RTE I had a letter asking me if my name was not an anglicization of Tadgh or Tague [–>Teigue] (Montague).

Current affairs programmes at RTE were increasingly being commissioned from independent producers (Irish Times).

RUC = Royal Ulster Constabulary (established 1922).

'We talked of McGivern who had been a policeman. R.U.C. But who quit to become an insurance consultant ... He was murdered a few days ago' (Kiely).

No evil British officers or sadistic RUC constables disturb the integrity of this fictional quarrel (Irish Times).

ruction Disturbance, riot, tumult (from 'insurrection'; the Insurrection of 1798 was often so called).

'I was out in the 'ruction of '98' (W. Wilde).

There was ructions in the theatre (O'Casey).

sally Willow (Irish *saileach* /sal'əx/, OE *sealh*).

Down by the salley gardens my love and I did meet (Yeats).

Building the cradle out of sallies and the cement-coloured rods of elder (McGahern).

Samhain November (Irish /saun'/); *Oíche Shamhna* /i:x'ə s'aunə/ = Hallowe'en (lit. 'night of November').

'It's a great rest I'll have now, and great sleeping in the long nights after Samhain' (Synge).

Samhain (Title, Yeats ed.).

Saorstát /seːrstaːt/siːrstaːt/ = Free State (Irish *saor* = free). *Saorstát Éireann* /eːr'ən/ was the Irish name of the Irish Free State from its establishment in 1922 until the Constitution of 1937, when the name was changed to –>Éire.

In our street general indignation was stirred by the case of Jack versus <u>Saorstat Eireann</u> (Behan).

Sassenach /sasənəx/ Saxon, Englishman.

'The Sassenach wants his morning –>rashers' (Joyce)

Irish music ... suffered more at the hands of –>gombeen men, like Moore, than through the suppressive activities of the Sassenach himself (Plunkett).

scald Vex, torment; esp. in the phrase 'to scald the heart'.

'He has me heartscalded' (Joyce).

Oh, how the vice of uncaringness had been hers ... Scalded by unredeeming tears, she fought through the undergrowth round the elder, twigs scornfully whipping at her face (Bowen).

'It would scald the heart out of him to be here and not able to take it [i.e. a boat] out' (Lavin).

scalteen Whiskey punch (from Irish *scailtín* /skalˈtʼiːnʼ/).

Von Pückler-Muskau was introduced to the Irish beverage <u>scalteen</u> after a hunt in –>Co. Tipperary, in the 1820s (Irish Times).

scoraíocht Social evening (Irish /skoriː(ə)xt/).

The twenty or thirty people assembled for the Sunday night scoraíocht (Behan).

She spoke of the old times and the scoraíocht / Back in Skibereen (Durcan).

scráidín

Scrawny, worthless thing or person (Irish *scráidín* /skra:d'i:n'/).

The scraidíns of farmers with their watery little hills (Kavanagh).

scraw

Grassy sod (from Irish *scraith* /skrah/).

He stooped and pulled a small scraw up with his hands like a man rescuing a drowning person by the hair of the head (Kavanagh).

seanad

/s'anəd/ = senate. *Seanad Éireann* /e:r'ən/ is one of the two Irish Houses of Parliament; members are called –>'senators'. See also –>Dáil, –>deputy, –>Oireachtas, –>TD.

'Delenda est Carthago' declaimed Senator Feargal Quinn in the Seanad on Wednesday during the debate on jobs (Irish Times).

semmit

Undershirt or vest (etym. doubtful; perhaps the same word as English 'samite', a fine silk cloth).

In socks and semmit and long woollen drawers (Kiely).

senator

Member of the Irish Senate or –>Seanad.

Some of the –>Fianna Fail lads were unhappy with ... the proposed restrictions on –>TDs and senators (Irish Times).

sept

Division of a nation or tribe; a clan (perhaps from a variant of 'sect', from Latin *secta* = following).

The eager accent of a free sept, / broken in the north, in resurrection (Paulin).

That is what –>Sinn Fein is. It is a sept within the greater tribe of Northern Catholics (Irish Times).

shamrock

Three-leaved clover (from Irish *seamróg* /s'amro:g/). A popular symbol of Ireland.

O −>Paddy dear and did you hear the news that's going round? / The shamrock is forbid by law to grow on Irish ground (Song).

Someone had sent me a shamrock and they were all delighted to get a bit ... Joe and Jock had it in their lapels (Behan).

shanachie Story-teller (from Irish *seanchaí* /s'anəxi:/).

The Shannaghie and the Callegh [−>cailleach] in the chimney corner, tell no more the tales and legends of other days (W. Wilde).

'Who should know better than yourself how stories are spun and woven, you the great shanachie of Connemara?' (G. Moore).

shandrydan A rickety old vehicle (first element from Irish *sean* /s'an/ = old).

The races were as gay as races could be ... Where all the people came from that thronged out of the town was a wonder; where all the vehicles ... barouches, and shandrydans (Thackeray).

'Did you see that old shandrydan of hers in the street a while ago, and a fellow on the box with a red beard on him like Robinson Crusoe?' (Somerville and Ross).

Shan Van Vocht Anglicised spelling of Irish *Sean Bhean Bhocht* /s'an v'an voxt/ = 'Poor Old Woman' (*Sean* = old, *Bhean* = woman, *Bhocht* = poor). One of many female symbols of Ireland. See Introduction and Appendix.

O the French are on the sea / says the Shan Van Vocht (Song).

'He dreams of what the Shan Van Vocht said in −>ninetyeight' (Shaw).

shaughraun Vagabond, vagabondage (from Irish *seachrán* /s'axra:n/ = straying, error; *seachránaí* /s'axra:ni:/ = wanderer). 'To be on the shaughraun' = to wander from place to place seeking work.

'[That salmon] was snared last night ... by Conn, the Shaughraun' (Boucicault).

When he was on the shaughraun (Joyce).

shawlie   Woman wearing large shawl, often a street vendor.

From the back ... she could have been a shawlie from Moore Street, pushing a pram of fish (Boylan).

Dublin shawlees, in the rare old days ... conversing civilly over cellar gratings after the pubs had closed (Irish Times).

shebeen   Low wayside public house, commonly unlicensed (from Irish *síbín* /s'i:b'i:n'/).

Country public house or shebeen, very rough and untidy (Synge).

We are encouraged to flee the austerity and rebuke of home for the comfort of strangers and the cordiality of the shebeen (Boylan).

The killing of Margaret Wright in a loyalist drinking den ... has focused attention on the nocturnal culture of the shebeens (Irish Times).

shee   Fairies (from Irish *sidhe* /s'i:/, pl. of *sióg* /s'i:o:g/). See also –>banshee and –>linnaun shee.

'They are saying you are a woman of the Sidhe, who rode into Donegal on a white horse, surrounded by birds for victory' (MacBride).

Adieu, sweet Angus, Maeve and Fand, / Ye plumed yet skinny Shee (Synge).

sheela-na-gig   Stone figure of a naked displaying female (perhaps from *Síle na gCiach*, personal name + gen. pl. of *cíoch* /k'i:x/ = breast: 'Sheila of the Paps').

> *Little wonder that Aidan was scared, for he had seen Cile-na-gCich. He had never heard ... of the obscene female image which was carven on the outside wall of certain chapels at that time* (Clarke).
>
> *Sheelagh na Gig at Kilpeck* (Title, Heaney).
>
> *There are lots of things which are hard to exactly define in art terms, as a sheela na gig* (Irish Times).

Shelta Ancient hybrid language spoken by –>travellers (perhaps from a form of 'Celtic').

> *A teacher who is engaged in collecting Shelta words from –>travelling children in County Wexford* (Irish Times).

she'nanigan Prankishness, mischief (etym. unknown).

> *He disapproved of Hunt Balls and similar shenanigans* (Farrell).

sheugh /ʃux/ Ditch, drain; also 'shugh' et al. (cf. Early Middle English 'sogh' = furrow; of uncertain origin).

> *In water and out of water, in shughs and out of shughs* (McLaverty).
>
> *Here's a wet sheugh / smells like a used sheath* (Paulin).

shift A woman's nightgown or chemise.

> *'Great queens ... and they with shiny silks on them the length of the day, and white shifts for the night'* (Synge).
>
> *'Even when we had our baths on Saturday nights they put shifts on all the girls.' — 'Put what on yer?' — 'A sort of sheet, you know'* (Behan).

shil'lelagh Cudgel, properly of oak (from the name of a village in County Wicklow famed for oak trees).

> *Shillelagh law did all engage, / And a row and a –>ruction soon began* (Song).

He is a huge powerful fierce-looking man of forty-five or so, and he carries a murderous looking shillelagh (Molloy).

Shinner Member of –>Sinn Fein.

'Some unsavoury characters have been spotted lurking in the grounds. Probably Shinners' (Farrell).

'I thought I'd heard it about that you were with the Shinners' (J. Johnston).

shite = 'shit'; the common form in Ireland. See also –>gobshite.

'Creatures were in the field ... their long swishing tails besmeared with stale shite (Joyce).

'O!' Mr Dedalus cried, giving vent to a hopeless groan [on hearing a piece of literary bombast], 'shite and onions' (perhaps an echo of 'tripe and onions') (Joyce).

'Little shite ... and you always were ... always ... from the minute you were born' (E. O'Brien).

shoneen Would-be (English) gentleman (from the Irish name *Seán* /s'a:n/ + dimin.).

'Those shoneens that are always hat in hand before any fellow with a handle to his name' (Joyce).

'A shoneen ... who aped the English gentry because he took them to be his betters' (Plunkett).

shugh See –>sheugh.

shut 'To get shut of' = to get rid of.

'I suppose he was glad to get shut of her' (Joyce).

He described the visit of the journalist and about sending him down to Fisher's Point to get shut of him (Plunkett).

side car	Two-wheeled horse-drawn vehicle, with seats on either side back to back. Also called a 'jaunting car', or an 'outsider' or 'outside car'.

Suddenly an outside car, one seat overturned to save the cushions from the wet, came careering up the –>avenue (G. Moore).

Mr Power whistled for an outsider (Joyce).

The dark blue sidecar, a red coat-of-arms on its tailboard and a grey horse between its shafts, came swirling towards her (M. Keane).

The bustling traffic of Dame Street ... the jaunting-cars with their nodding horses (Farrell). |
| **Sidhe** | See –>shee. |
| **Sile-na-Gig** | See –>sheela-na-gig. |
| **Sinn Fein** | The political wing of the –>IRA (Irish *sinn* /s'in'/ = we, us + *féin* /f'e:n'/ = -self).

Exploratory talks between the British government and Sinn Fein representatives (Irish Times). |
| **Six Counties** | The north-eastern counties of Antrim, Armagh, Down, Fermanagh, Londonderry and Tyrone, which since 1920 have made up the separate state of Northern Ireland within the United Kingdom. See also –>Ulster, –>Thirty-two Counties, and –> Twenty-six Counties.

He wanted to ship anything from a Six Counties' port because he wanted to sail into a British port with a British Customs manifest (Behan).

I broke into a Belfast accent which made the other officer hoot with delight ... 'Up the Six Counties!' he said (O'Connor). |
| **skean** | Knife (from Irish *scian* /s'k'iən/). |

A Cubit at least / The length of their skeans (Swift).

skelp To beat or smack (probably of Scandinavian origin). Also a noun.

'"Skelp her, ye big brute!" says I. "What good's in ye that ye aren't able to skelp her?"' The yell and the histrionic flourish of his stick with which Slipper delivered this incident brought down the house. Leigh Kelway [an Englishman] was sufficiently moved to ask me in an undertone if 'skelp' was a local term (Somerville and Ross).

'Did you see the skelp he gave him?' (D. Johnston).

sláinte A common toast (Irish *sláinte* /sla:n't'ə/ = health).

Come fill up all neighbours, fill high to the brim, / And cry slainte to freedom again and again (Kickham).

She said 'Cheers' and he 'Slainte' (MacLaverty).

slane Turf spade (from Irish *sleán* /s'l'a:n/).

The walls ... were lined with –>turf, the side-walls with the regular 'slane' turf, which looked like brick-work blackened with smoke, and the end wall with the rougher and somewhat shapeless 'hand-turf' (Kickham).

Barney Horish, leaning on his slean (Montague).

sleiveen Mean, sly fellow; rogue (from Irish *slíbhín* /s'l'i:v'i:n'/, probably from *sliabh* /s'l'iəv/ = mountain + dimin.).

Sleiveens were all his race (Yeats).

Like the –>cute old sleeveen that I am where anything connected with eating and drinking are concerned (Behan)

sliotar Ball used in –>hurling (from Irish *sliotar* /s'l'itər/).

Cú Chulainn ... drove a <u>sliotar</u> down the hound's throat and then beat it over the head with a ->hurley stick (O'Connor).

Nothing but mountains and, barely visible, a handful of men pucking sliotars on the heathery hill (Irish Times).

slob Mud, esp. soft mud on sea-shore (from Irish *slaba* /slabə/ = mud); 'slobland' = muddy ground. Also used of slovenly persons.

'Did she refuse him?' Grace asked. 'No, miss; she was fond uv [= of] the slob — but she hadn't the fortune' (Kickham).

Molly was about twenty years old, a soft, flat slob of a girl (Kavanagh).

Primal light, soaked green / the slob mud / and a salt tang (Paulin).

The slow curve of the coastline going ... to the sloblands and Wexford town (Toibin).

sma'han Nip, small amount (from Irish *smeachán* /sm'axa:n/).
'We'll just have one little smahan more' (Joyce).

smithereen Fragment, small bit.

'Tis on'y the mercy of God ... that he doesn't make smithereens uv [= of] himself [by falling down from a tree]' (Kickham).

'You're a bit of all right, aren't you?' 'A smithereen' (Beckett).

Dropping the wine bottle on top of the goblet, splitting it into smithereens (White).

smoored A fire is 'smoored' by being buried in ash (from Irish *smúr* /smu:r/ = ash, soot).

You sifted the smoored ashes / to blow / a fire's sleeping remains / back to life (Montague).

smug To fondle, to play at sex.

What did that mean about the smugging in the square? Why did the five fellows out of the higher line run away for that? (Joyce).

so Commonly used in a final position, meaning 'then', 'in that case', etc.
'D'you want a slice of cake, Elmer?' ... 'Is it cherry?' Elmer said. 'It is.' 'I'll take a slice so' (Trevor).

'Give me directions so' (Brady).

soda bread Bread made with baking soda.

Soon he was wearily masticating soda bread sandwiches (Farrell).

A plate of buttered soda bread was passed about (McGahern).

soft day Day of gentle rain or drizzle (cf. Irish *bog*, which means both 'soft' and 'wet').

'After three / Or four days with rain falling gods decree / A soft kind morning on the hills' (Synge).

The locals, polite and deferential. Soft day, your honour, –>sure the trout will be –>lepping (Flanagan).

sog(g)art Priest (from Irish *sagart* /sagərt/). 'Soggart Aroon' = 'beloved priest'; cf. –>aroon.

'Axe [= ask] to see the young sogarth' (Carleton).

Who was it led the van, Soggart Aroon? / Since the fight first began, Soggart Aroon? (Song)

Soldier's Song Ireland's National Anthem. See –>Amhrán na bhFiann.

Once an imperial garrison / Drank here to a king: / Today's toast is republican, / We sing 'A Soldier's Song' (R. Murphy).

'Now that they've stood up like fools for the Soldier's Song they can all go home in peace' (McGahern).

sonsy Fine-looking, healthy (cf. Irish *sonas* /sonəs/ = good fortune).

'*A sonsy, strong woman*' (Kiely).

sorra Interjection with negative implication (suggested etymologies: 'sirrah' ('sir'); 'sorry'; 'sorrow'; Irish *sáraigh* = to violate, frustrate, or *sárú* = violation, frustration).

'Sorrow a one that I know of has a word to say in the matter' (Trollope).

'Sorra much business he laves [= leaves] afther him wherever he'll go' (Somerville and Ross).

'Sorry the night that was the decision' (T. Murphy).

souper Protestant seeking to make proselytes by dispensing soup in charity.

'–>Sure you don't think he'd turn souper and marry her in a Protestant church?' (Lady Gregory).

'They're Governmint schools. Run be [by] the English, heathen schools, to drag away innocent Irish childer [= children]. Souper schools!' (Kilroy).

spalpeen Labourer who travelled about in the autumn seeking employment from farmers. Now usually = a rascal (from Irish *spailpín* /spal'p'i:n'/).

For the next few years he wandered annually, either as <u>spailpín</u> or schoolmaster (Corkery).

I encountered a half-dozen or so spalpeens, wandering labourers who had perhaps drifted to Killala for the approaching harvest (Flanagan).

spawg Large clumsy foot (from Irish *spág* /spa:g/).

'Look at the young guttersnipe behind him ... Taking off [= imitating] his flat spaugs and the walk' (Joyce).

'Soft Willie inside, quiet by the hearth, but she knew he'd be able, the spawgs of hands he had on him' (T. Murphy).

splinter Slip of bog-deal, dipped in tallow and used as a candle.

His two little boys were roasting potatoes in the ashes, while his rosy daughter held a splinter to her mother (Croker).

'A splinter of bog-wood, lurid in the smoke, supplied us with light for our evening meal' (Corkery).

spoiled Said of nuns and priests who return to lay life.

He had heard his father say that she was a spoiled nun and that she had come out of the convent (Joyce).

A spoiled priest turned –>hedge schoolmaster (Flanagan).

squireen Petty squire, small land-owner (from English 'squire' + Irish dimin.).

In the neighbourhood ... there were several squireens, or little squires ... Busy and loud about small matters ... trying upon every occasion, public or private, to push themselves forward, to the annoyance of their superiors, and the terror of those below them (Edgeworth).

He had the look of a Mayo squireen, a man with a jockey's slender, nervous frame, and a face like a hatchet, narrow and triangular (Flanagan).

standing stone Large block of stone set upright; a menhir, monolith.

Bury me under a standing stone beside a well or spring (Montague).

A standing stone and a well weathered –>Celtic Cross, rubbed by cattle perhaps, were the only monuments to the sixth century saint (Irish Times).

stare   Starling.

O honey bees, / Come build in the empty house of the stare (Yeats).

station¹   Holy place visited by pilgrims (as in the name Station Island on Lough Derg in County Donegal, also known as St. Patrick's Purgatory); also each unit that is visited.

Making their way to the several 'stations' upon the hill (Thackeray).

'You'd have thought that Anahorish School / was purgatory enough for any man,' / I said. 'You've done your station' (Heaney).

station²   One of the 'Stations of the Cross': the series of images representing successive incidents of the Passion of Christ, placed in a church in order to be visited for meditation or prayer.

There were fourteen stations of the cross depicting the route to Calvary, occupying both main walls (E. O'Brien).

One of the Stations shows Symon of Cyrene helping Jesus to carry the Cross (Devlin).

station³   The visit of a priest to selected households at Easter and Christmas, to give those in the neighbourhood the opportunity of confession.

'The station is at Mr. Reilly's to-day' (Kickham).

Farmers' sons themselves, those priests, but risen now in the world a bit, holding stations in the homes of the graziers and auctioneers and land agents (Flanagan).

GLOSSARY

stirabout Porridge, gruel.

'We had nothing to eat at that time,' he said, 'but milk and stirabout and potatoes' (Synge).

'He's really an awful bother ... forcing Eva to eat the stirabout' (Joyce).

stook Peak (from Irish *stuaic* /stuək/).

There used to be great gatherings of people and great dancings on the stooks over the head of Inch (Synge).

stotious Drunk (perhaps mock-Latin). Also 'stoshus', 'stocious' et al.

'The poor thing is <u>stoshus</u>!' cried one of the maids (Farrell).

Letty had said her brother-in-law was drinking. 'Stotious,' Mrs Dallon pronounced (Trevor).

strap Harlot, termagant (from Irish *straip* /strap'/).

'You infernal old strap!' shouted he, as he clutched a handful of bottles on the table near him, and flung them at the nurse (Lover).

'You be damned you lying strap' (Joyce).

stravage /stra ǀ veig/. To stroll or wander about; also 'stravague' et al. (from OFr. *estravaguer*, from Latin *extravagari*).

'Go in an' tell him I'm sthravagin' outside till he's soft' (Boucicault).

streel Slattern, slovenly-looking person; also file, ragged line (from Irish *sraoill* /sri:l'/ = slattern, *sraoillín* /sri:l'i:n'/ = file). Adj.: streelish.

Nobody would have such a streel as she was reputed to be (Fitzmaurice).

The children, lice-ridden and ashen with hunger, walked back and forth to the town to beg in streels of four or five holding hands across the width of the common highway (Kilroy).

Maids were all alike, streelish, always from the mountains (E. O'Brien).

streeleen Flow of discourse (perhaps from Irish *sraoillín* /sri:l'i:n'/, cf. preceding entry).

'You'd have as much talk and streeleen, I'm thinking, as Owen Roe O'Sullivan and the poets of Dingle Bay' (Synge).

strippen The last and richest milk that comes from a cow at a milking.

'Put your lips to that jug; there's only the sthrippens left' (Boucicault).

strong Wealthy (said of farmers).

There were ... a vast number of strong farmers, with bursting granaries and immense –>haggards (Carleton).

The captain ... fulfilled the final requirement of the Irish strong farmer by having a son studying for the priesthood in Maynooth (Kiely).

su'gan Rope of hay or straw (from Irish *súgán* /su:ga:n/).

'Lead him home with a sugan the way you'd lead a bleating goat' (Joyce).

These old men walked on the summer road / sugán belts and long black coats / with big –>ashplants (Hartnett).

Mulcaire was left a cripple ... / Tied to a sugawn chair (Kennelly).

Sunday traveller Person travelling on Sundays, who was formerly exempt from licensing laws. See also –>bona fide.

A door consecrated to the unobtrusive visits of so-called 'Sunday travellers' (Somerville and Ross).

sup A small amount of liquid; a drink. 'Sup and shelter' = board and lodging.

'Whenever he sees I've a sup taken' (Joyce).

'Could nothing be done about this?' he asked, seeing water under the bottom boards of the boat. It was only a small sup (Lavin).

In many a village they have been given sup and shelter while they tell their story (Flanagan).

sure Common opening word in a sentence.

When Irish eyes are smiling, / Sure it's like a morn in Spring (Song).

'Sure isn't our own Grania a –>class of a goddess' (Friel).

swaddler Wesleyan preacher; a hypocrite. Used derogatorily of Catholics who converted to Protestantism for material gain.

'Is he a jew or a gentile or a holy Roman or a swaddler or what the hell is he?' (Joyce).

Sweep The Irish Sweeps handicap chase, a horse race.

'An old –>I.R.A man with an agency in the Sweep' (Behan).

Tague See –>Teigue.

Taig See –>Teigue.

Táin The *Táin Bó Cúailnge* /taːnʹ boː kuːliŋʹə/ = the Cattle Raid of Cooley; Ireland's best known heroic epic, often called merely the 'Táin'.

> *One of the major elements of the <u>Táin</u> is its topography* (Kinsella).
>
> *Bob Dylan and his Band – / And a hundred thousand fans – / Made noise that out-Táined the Táin* (Durcan).

tally woman   Young woman from the tenantry who served as mistress to a member of the landowning class and was paid off, or married off, when she became pregnant (from 'tally' in the sense 'agreement').

> *As for the gentry, the legends that clung about them were sulphurous — of riotous parties, and of –>squireens with their tally women* (Flanagan).

Tan   See –>Black and Tans.

Tan War   = The –>War of Independence. See also –>Black and Tans.

Tanaiste   Deputy prime minister (from Irish *tánaiste* /taːnəsˈtʲə/ = heir presumptive, tanist).

> *Next to him [i.e. the captain] do they Chose the next of blood to be Tanist, who shall next succeed him* (Spenser).
>
> *The Tanaiste and Minister for Foreign Affairs told the –>Dail yesterday that the international response to the Joint Declaration had been extremely gratifying* (Irish Times).

Taoiseach   Prime Minister (from Irish *taoiseach* /tiːsˈəx/ = chief, ruler).

> *The Taoiseach and the British Prime Minister meet in two weeks time* (Irish Times).

tare   See –>tear.

tavered   Exhausted.

> *Robbie was merciful enough to allow the tavered horse to walk* (Kiely).

Teague See –>Teigue.

tear = English 'tear' /tiə/; formerly often pronounced /tæə/ in Ireland and spelt 'tare' i.a. in the oaths 'Tare an' ages' and 'Tare an' 'ounds' (allegedly derived from 'Tears and Aches' and 'Tears and Wounds' of Christ). See also –>ouns.

'Oh – tare an' ages – what'll I do?' (Boucicault).

'Tear and 'ounds Misther Lord Chief Justice! ... and are ye niver going to opin them big doors?' (Trollope).

Teigue /teig/ Also 'Tague', 'Taig' et al., Irish *Tadhg* /te:g/; the Irish name corresponding to the English 'Timothy'. An early name for an Irish servant in English plays (see Appendix), nowadays a sectarian term for 'Catholic' in Northern Ireland.

Teigue in his green coat rides to war (R. Murphy).

'That's what we think of Roman Catholics. There's something spooky about them. Taigs' (MacLaverty).

'They were all definitely –>Prods. I'm the only Tague here' (Reid).

TD Member of the –>Dáil (abbr. of Irish *Teachta Dála* /t'axtə da;lə/; Irish *teachta* = messenger).

'I know that the T.D.'s and the ministers above in –>Dail Eireann will be cryin' their eyes out after I'm gone' (J. B. Keane).

Given the high turnover of TDs, is it not reasonable for a TD to keep an eye on 'life after politics'? (Irish Times).

teem To strain or pour off liquid (from Irish *taom* /ti:m/, from ON *tæma* = to empty).

'Give us a hand to teem the pot' (Kavanagh).

tenement Usually a large and formerly elegant house, run down and divided into flats.

I was born in a Georgian house that had gone to rack and ruin as a tenement (Behan).

'You go round looking like an old hag from the tenements' (Murdoch).

termon well Well belonging to a religious foundation (from Irish *tearmann* /t'arəmən/ = sanctuary).

I dip the termon-well for drink / And pull the sloe for bread (Campbell).

the The definite article + surname = the head of a clan or family.

Sing of the O'Rahilly, / Do not deny his right; / Sing a 'the' before his name (Colum).

He was The MacDermott, chief of one of the oldest and proudest families in Irish history (Flanagan).

thirteen Name formerly current in Ireland for the English silver shilling, which was worth 13 pence of the Irish copper currency before the two currencies were amalgamated in 1821.

Thousands of little men and women ... were pelting one another with golden guineas and lily-white thirteens (Croker).

'Dog chape [= cheap], at six thirteens' (Hall).

Thirty-two Counties The whole of Ireland, including both North and South. See also –>Six Counties and –> Twenty-six Counties.

'Myself and my colleague here,' I explained, 'have come up [i.e. to Belfast] from Dublin today to do a lawful job of work for the Irish Lights, which is a Thirty-Two County organisation [controlling the lighthouses of Ireland]' (Behan).

thrawn	Twisted, misshapen; obstinate (pp. of 'thraw', variant of 'throw').
	There were no thrawn, black-faced mountain sheep on the grass (Kiely).
	If he was thrawn enough to reject that advice (Kiely).
thrawneen	See –>traneen.
tilly	Extra measure (from Irish *tuilleadh* /tilˈə/).
	She poured again a measure full and a tilly (Joyce).
	The women constantly grumbling that Mr. Divene always gave them a betther tilly, so he did (O'Casey).
tinker	One of a group of people with no fixed abode, perhaps descended from wandering craftsmen who mended pots, etc. ('tinkers'); now often derogatory. Also –>'traveller', 'travelling people' or, more officially, 'itinerants'.
	One day a tinker and his wife came to the door (Lewis).
	Her voice had a real tinker whine to it (J. Johnston).
	Among the dust-heaps bands of tinkers scavenged for scrap metal (Banville).
top of the morning	Well-worn greeting that became a notorious Stage Irishism. See Appendix.
	'The top o' the morning to my –>colleen!' (Hall)
	The words — 'The top of the morning to you, Miss Grace,' suggested the idea that Father Hannigan affected the phraseology of the peasantry (Kickham).
	'Surely a fellow-countryman may pass you the top of the morning without offence ...' — 'The top of the morning! Did he call you the –>broth of a boy?' (Shaw).
townland	Division of land of varying extent.

'In the townland of Garrynapeaka, in the district of Inchigeela, in the parish of Iveleary, in the barony of West Muskerry, in the county of Cork, in the –>province of Munster' – as he magniloquently styles his address, lives the Tailor (Cross).

'I the fright of seven townlands for my biting tongue' (Synge).

A townland that bordered on other townlands of equal indistinctiveness (E. O'Brien).

traneen Straw; insignificant trifle (from Irish *tráithnín* /tra:hn'i:n'/).

'The field itself not worth a traneen' (Hall).

'I wouldn't give a thraneen for a lad hadn't a mighty spirit in him' (Synge).
Rita puts a thrawneen in my mouth, takes the other end in hers and dares me to race her to the knob in the centre (Higgins).

traveller One of a group of people with no fixed abode. Also called 'travelling people', or, more officially, 'itinerants'; also –>'tinkers'.

The gypsies ... hadn't been real romany gypsies but –>tinkers or travelling people from the west of Ireland (Kiely).

When the children heard, they gathered together / And in a trice were / Stalking the little weary traveller (Kennelly).

Task force calls for traveller accomodation (Headline, Irish Times).

travelling people See preceding entry.

Treaty The Anglo-Irish Treaty of 1921.

He left Ireland when the Treaty was signed (Iremonger trans.).

GLOSSARY

After the Treaty / Had brought civil war to this fisherman's town (R. Murphy).

trews Close fitting hose or breeches (apparently the same word as 'trousers'; from Irish *triús* /t'r'u:s/). Trews were part of the characteristic dress worn by Irishmen on the early stage; see Appendix.

He wore a long unsleeved garment of recently flayed oxhide ... Beneath this he wore trews of deerskin, roughly stitched with gut (Joyce).

All he ever got to do [instead of acting properly himself] was stand around in sackcloth trews and a tunic that smelled of someone else's sweat (Banville).

tricolour Since 1922, the green-white-orange flag of Ireland.

The Republican Tricolour of Orange, White and Green was flying from the roof of the General Post Office (O'Duffy).

The television news came on ... Moore watched an image of the Union Jack and the Irish tricolour spring onto the screen (Brady).

The Tricolour as a tribal colour was unknown before 1916 (Irish Times).

Troubles Periods of rebellion or civil strife. Often used of the violence accompanying the emergence of the ->Irish Free State; more recently of the violence in Northern Ireland.

The bomb was in his possession since the time of the Troubles (Plunkett).

'Then there was the Troubles, of course. After 'sixty-nine people just stopped coming' (MacLaverty).

The general who commanded the British forces during the Troubles in the 1920s (Irish Times).

turbary The right of cutting ->turf; a piece of land where turf is cut.

131

'Would you give me the red cow you have ... and a load of dung at Michaelmas, and turbary upon the western hill?' (Synge).

State machines are cutting ->turf for miles / That furnaces may stop the centuries / Of turbary (Clarke).

Beyond the turbary, with its mud-fringed, pear-shaped ->bog pool (Kiely).

turf   Peat cut for use as fuel, commonly used all over Ireland until recently.

The stack of turf, the lamp to light, / The good earth wall of a winter's night (O'Connor trans.).

The smell of the town was of turf-smoke mainly, acrid in the damp air (Trevor).

Twenty-six Counties   Ireland with the exception of the six north-eastern counties, which became Northern Ireland by the Government of Ireland Act, 1920. See also –>Six Counties and –>Thirty-two Counties.

'In the Free State, or the Twenty-six Counties, or whatever you like to call it' (Behan).

uilleann pipes   Irish bagpipes; also 'elbow', 'onion', 'woollen', 'alien', 'villein' et al. (Irish *uillinn* /il'ən'/, gen. *uilleann* = elbow). See also –>piper.

A snake charmer with Uileann pipes (Behan).

The broader interpretation is saluted by Sean Og Potts (uilleann pipes), Sean Ryan (whistle) and Jerry O'Connor (banjo) (Irish Times).

'I heard you on a radio programme saying you were going to have this bloke playing at your funeral,' he began. 'A bagpiper of some sort.' 'An uileann piper called Liam O Flionn,' I said (Irish Times).

ullagone   Exclamation of sorrow, lamentation; also 'hullagone', 'ologoan' et al. (imitative). Also verb.

Oh-roh! with a great hullagone! (O'Riada trans.).

We could drink undisturbed by his ullagoning about his graceless son (Kiely).

'Sit up all night ologroan-ing and ologoaning' (S. O'Faolain).

ullaloo   See –>whillaluh.

Ulster   One of the four historical provinces of Ireland (the others being Munster, Leinster, and Connacht /kɔnəxt/); of Ulster's nine counties, six were established as Northern Ireland under the Government of Ireland Act, 1920. Northern Ireland continued to be called Ulster colloquially, and the name is used officially in such bodies as the Royal Ulster Constabulary, the –>RUC. See also –>Six Counties.

The smoking chimneys hint / At prosperity round the corner / But they make their Ulster linen from foreign lint / And the money that comes in goes out to make more money (MacNeice).

The border partitions Ulster more than it does Ireland as a whole (Behan).

Union[1]   'The Union' usually refers to the Act of Union between Great Britain and Ireland, 1800.

Dublin such as it appeared to her soon after the union (Edgeworth).

The 1770s ... witnessed ... the years of rebellion which led to the Union (Flanagan).

union[2]   Workhouse.

In Wicklow, as in the rest of Ireland, the union, though it is a home of refuge for the tramps and –>tinkers, is looked upon with supreme horror by the –>peasants (Synge).

'Pack you off to the Union the minute you showed a sign of feebleness' (Plunkett).

visiting house A house where neighbours met to exchange gossip and tell stories.

The Visiting House (Title, Molloy).

Volunteers May refer spec. to the Irish Volunteers of the 18th century, or to the movement founded 1913 that in 1920 became the Irish Republican Army, the –>IRA.

Yeomanry corps of infantry and cavalry, which coalesced into an army known as the Volunteers (Flanagan).

The fortification was manned by five men in the grey-green uniform of the Volunteers (O'Duffy).

wake The watching of the dead from death to burial, usually accompanied by drinking and festivities. Also verb.

'Do not spread food to call strangers / To the wakes that shall be to-morrow' (Yeats).

'I never seen a wake till this day with fine spirits, and good tobacco, and the best of pipes, and no one to taste them but a woman only' (Synge).

'We were disgraced forever, if you were waked with less than two half barrels' (Molloy).

wan = one, reflecting a non-Standard pronunciation; in the Dublin area the vowel approaches [a].

'–>Begor, I'm glad we have him, as I was afeard [= afraid] there'd be no wan to talk to the ladies' (Kickham).

I remember ... hearing an oul' wan [–>ould] moaning to my mother (Behan).

War of Independence Guerilla warfare against the British authorities, 1919-1921; also called the 'Anglo-Irish War' or the 'Tan War'.

The years his father was most proud of were the years of the War of Independence when he was the commander of a small army of men on the run (McGahern).

Whytescourt House was burned down during the War of Independence (Kilroy),

His family's involvement in 1916 and the War of Independence (Tóibín).

warrant Expert. 'A great warrant to' = a great hand at doing something.

She was a great warrant to scold (O'Connor).

Peadar was old, too, a proper crow in clothes he was, but he was a great warrant to eke out his stories (MacMahon).

water To 'cross' or 'go across' the water = to go abroad, usually to England.

Whether he had crossed the water or was still in Ireland was for some time unknown (Le Fanu).

He never gets tired of advising people to go across the water and not be wasting their lives here (Iremonger trans.).

west = both 'west' and 'back' (trans. of Irish *siar* /s'iər/, both meanings).

'Move west a small piece, Mary Jack, if you please,' said a voluminous matron [in the train] (Somerville and Ross).

West Briton Pro-British Irishman.

A man sitting opposite to him in the railway carriage began to lament that Queen Victoria had not been received with more profuse expressions of loyalty; [he] took this West Briton very gently at first (G. Moore).

'Well, I'm ashamed of you,' said Miss Ivors frankly. 'To say you'd write for a rag like that [i.e. The Daily Express]. I didn't think you were a West Briton' (Joyce).

The Jesuits and Dominicans ... were seen as providers of schools for West Britons (McGahern).

whillaluh Funeral lament; also 'ullaloo' et al. (imitative).

Such a fine whillaluh! you might have heard it to the farthest end of the county (Edgeworth).

Whiteboys Agrarian secret society in the 18th century; members wore white shirts over their other clothes to identify them at night. See also –>Ribbonmen.

Some Whiteboys were there then, they were fighting the English (Iremonger trans.).

'Draw a coffin [on the letter], is what the Whiteboys used to do in the old days' (Flanagan).

white haired Favourite; also '–>white headed'. See also –>bawn².

'I was a fine brave boy, the pride of my –>ould mother, her white haired darlin'' (Boucicault).

white headed Favourite; also '–>white haired'. See also –>bawn².

'He was ever my white-headed boy' (Edgeworth).

The Whiteheaded Boy (Title, Robinson).

wild geese Esp. used about those Irishmen who left the country after the Battle of Limerick in 1691.

Was it for this the wild geese spread / The grey wing upon every tide (Yeats).

The wild geese are gone, but the goslings are flying; / The young men of twenty are leaving the land (J. B. Keane).

wisha Variant of –>musha.

'Wisha, I'll do that for you, child,' she said meekly (O'Connor).

GLOSSARY

'How serious is this, Maura?' 'Wisha, you know how they fib you. I think they don't know' (Brady).

wolfhound Breed of large dog kept for hunting wolves, traditionally associated with the heroes of Ancient Ireland.

A wolfhound sits under a wild ash / Licking the wound in a dead ensign's neck (R. Murphy).

Wolfhounds, lean as models, / At their urgent heels (Montague).

wren boys Young lads, often wearing straw masks, who went round from house to house on St. Stephen's Day (December 26th) carrying a wren they had killed, and demanding money or drinks.

They are only called wren boys who carry the wren in a holly bush decorated with ribbons from house to house on St. Stephen's Day; and many who hunt the wren do not join in this part of the proceedings (Kickham).

'Wren boys,' Tom said. 'They sing "The wren, the wren, the king of all birds." It is all cheerful, but a bit frightening' (Flanagan).

ya'hoo A brutish person (Swift's name for a race of man-like brutes in *Gulliver's Travels*).

The fore-feet of the Yahoo differed from my hands in nothing else but the length of the nails, the coarseness and brownness of the palms, and the hairiness of the backs (Swift).

Black berets and dark glasses are the regimental badges of the Bombomb Yahoos (Kiely).

'I thought you were some yahoo coming for my aul' fella [= old fellow]' (E. O'Brien).

yellow meal Flour made from maize.

It was yellow meal that she had dampened with sugared water and this she kneaded with her fingers into small pellets (Kilroy).

Last weekend my son brought me back two different types of yellow meal from a shop in Killorglin where it is still being sold, a tradition which must date back almost to –>Famine times (Irish Times).

yerra	Interjection used at beginning of a sentence (from the interjection –>*arrah* preceded by *a Dhia* /ə ɣ'iə/ = O God).

'A free Ireland!' Tully said. 'Yerrah, isn't freedom for the poor country what we all want?' (Flanagan).

'Yerra, 'tis nothing,' said I, jovial and Irish (Behan).

yez	= you (pl.); also 'yous', 'yis'.

'Let me go this minute, every one of yez' (Le Fanu).

'Are yous goin' to keep us waitin' for yous all night?' (O'Casey).

'You correct me without insulting me. I write "yez" meaning "you all", and you just say "Wouldn't it be better to put you all, it might be clearer"...' (Binchy).

'Will yis do a message [= an errand] for me, girls?' (Doyle).

yis	See –>yez.

yoke	Gadget, vehicle, object, 'thingummy'.

'You'd want to keep that yoke there from getting wet through, Your Grace,' said one of the men, indicating the crozier that had fallen on the boards (Lavin).

'Out there on the sea ... everything is so big and man is just a tiny yoke of a thing' (Macken).

'A little yoke for coring apples' (Trevor).

yous	See –>yez.

APPENDIX

A Note on Stage Irishmen and Patriotic Images

The popular image of the Irish is widely familiar in the crude caricatures of present-day cartoons and joke-books: slovenly 'bog-trotters' with a gift for honeyed words, a taste for strong drink, and a penchant for hand-to-hand fighting. Cardboard cut-outs like this owe a good deal to theatrical stereotyping; they are first cousins, as it were, of the *Stage Irishman*, that larger-than-life compound of supposed national characteristics belonging to the black and white world of popular drama. Though the stereotype was originally created for the benefit of English audiences, it was in fact not confined to fiction, on or off the stage. By the 19th century it had become a well-established national image that many culturally displaced Irish immigrants abroad found themselves conforming to, and which their new neighbours readily endorsed.

Irish characters had been known to English playgoers since the 16th century. In the Elizabethan theatre their appearance alone would have been enough to identify them: close-fitting trousers or *trews*, a shaggy mop of hair (*glib*), and an all-enveloping mantle. In the pages of *Punch* three centuries later the 'typical' Irishman was also recognisable on sight, now equipped with an old battered hat (*caubeen*), a clay pipe (*dudeen*), and a murderous looking cudgel, a *shillelagh*.

18th and 19th century stereotypes

After the Restoration, Irishmen had become stock characters in the English theatre, where they were always good for a laugh, whether as fortune-hunting officers or their oafish servants. They would be quick to reach for their sword or their shillelagh, ingratiating, talkative, gullible, fond of the ladies and often over-fond of whiskey (which was a strange drink to the English, who drank brandy if they were well off, gin if they were not). Their speech immediately placed them as 'different', often ridiculously so; not only their accent or *brogue*, but also their use of non-Standard words and turns of phrase, and a sentence structure that owed more to Irish (Gaelic) than English usage. They were, moreover, habitually guilty of mispronunciations and, especially after 1700, of *bulls* – expressions involving a ludicrous inconsistency of the type *What has posterity ever done for me?* Logical blunders like this were so often associated with the Irish that they are still known as 'Irish' bulls.

Certain Irish character-types came into prominence in the theatre over the years, depending a good deal on the actors who personified them. In the 19th century, the dashing but impoverished officer of earlier plays had all but disappeared, and his comic servant had become a lovable rogue whose quick wit often saved the day for the hapless lovers of the play's intrigue. Dion Boucicault's Irish plays of the 1860s and 70s are notable (and much-abused) examples of sentimental melodrama centering on this rogue-type; resourceful rogues like his Myles-na-Coppaleen ('Myles of the Little Horses') are quite different from the bumbling Irish louts commonly projected in early 19th century writing, epitomised in the figure of the good-natured bumpkin Handy Andy in Samuel Lover's novel of that name.

In our own century, Brendan Behan added a postscript to the notion of Stage Irishman, so to speak, by gaining media acclaim as a living example of the Roaring Irish Boy.

Stage Irishisms

The Stage Irish vocabulary also changed with the times, and many expressions that were once the stock-in-trade of the Stage Irishman gradually fell out of use. This happened e.g. to *Joy* or *Dear Joy*; around 1700, Irish characters used this mode of address so often that for a time any Irishman might jokingly be called *a dear-joy*.

19th century novels and tales of Irish life aimed at the English market are a storehouse of clichés of what is sometimes called the *Faix and Begorra* type, *Faix* ('faith') and *Begorra* ('by God') being among the expressions that were most commonly used to label a person 'Irish'. The convention of linguistic markers has persisted well into our own century in any rough-and-ready portrayal of Irish characters – in the ubiquitous *Mick's* and *Paddy's* of anti-Irish jokes, for instance, and in the innumerable barefoot *colleens* (*Kathleen, Eileen, Mary*) of sentimental song albums, which are full of *Sure*'s and *Mavourneen*'s ('my dear') and the like. Many popular hibernicisms were lambasted by G. B. Shaw in *John Bull's Other Island* (1904), which has a Stage Irishman to end all Stage Irishmen; his speech is peppered with *Sure*'s and *Begorra*'s, and he gladly uses expressions that had by then become notoriously stagey: *a broth of a boy* and *top o' the morning*.

Counter-images

The hostile or patronizing English attitude epitomized by the Stage Irishman contributed not a little to the birth of a potent native counter-image: Ireland not as the backward, feckless country that she appeared to prejudiced English eyes, but a 'land of saints and scholars' with a proud early history of her own and a heroic, pre-Christian literature that could vie with that of Greece and Rome. Antiquarian zeal of the late 18th and the 19th century did much to encourage this view, and in poetry Ireland itself was sometimes regarded with an almost religious fervour. For reasons of secrecy the country had long been worshipped in various guises; best known is perhaps that of a rose which was at the same time a beautiful girl, Dark Rosaleen, *Roisín Dubh* /ros'i:n' duv/. Other female incarnations of Ireland are *Kathleen ni Houlihan* /hu:lihan/ (*ni* = daughter of), and the *Shan Van Vocht*, the poor old woman walking the roads, lamenting the loss of her 'four beautiful green fields' (the provinces Ulster, Munster, Leinster, and Connacht /kɔnəxt/).

Much of this imagery quickly degenerated into the rhetorical clichés of political balladmaking. To-day it is found chiefly in the language of marketing and tourism, along with the tangible national symbols that proliferated in the last century – shamrocks, round towers, Celtic crosses, and many others. The Irish harp (alone, perhaps, among these icons) still has a dignity of its own, being the official emblem of Ireland.

ILLUSTRATIONS

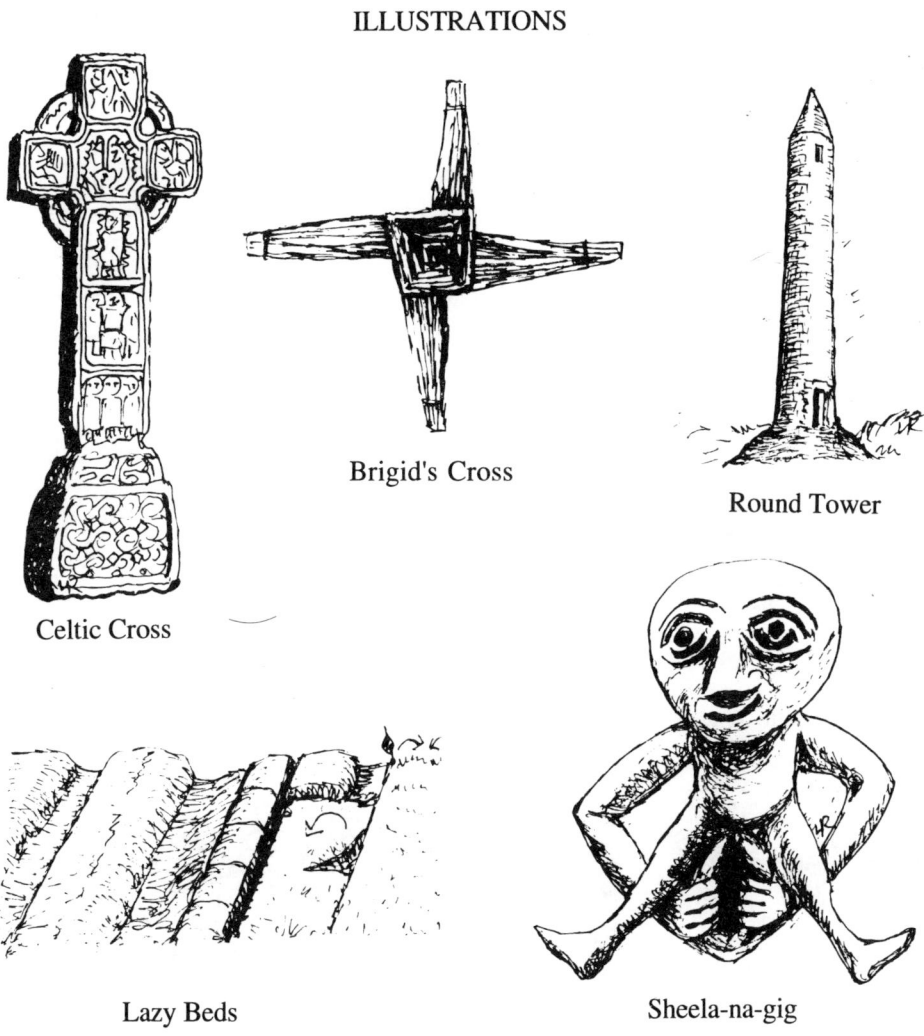

Celtic Cross

Brigid's Cross

Round Tower

Lazy Beds

Sheela-na-gig

Side Car

Ogham Stone

Martello Tower

Beehive Hut

Cromlech

Curragh

AUTHORS QUOTED

Allingham, William, 1824-89
Banville, John, 1948-
Barrington, Sir Jonah, 1760-1834
Beckett, Samuel, 1906-89
Behan, Brendan, 1923-64
Binchy, Maeve, 1940-
Boland, Eavan, 1944-
Bolger, Dermot, 1959-
Boucicault, Dion, 1820?-90
Boylan, Clare, 1948-
Bowen, Elizabeth, 1899-1973
Brady, John, 1955-
Brown, Christy, 1932-81
Campbell, Joseph, 1879-1944
Carleton, William, 1794-1869
Clarke, Austin, 1896-1974
Colum, Padraig, 1881-1972
Corkery, Daniel, 1878-1964
Croker, T. Crofton, 1798-1854
Cronin, Anthony, 1926-
Cross, Eric, 1903-80
Daly, Ita, 1945-
Davis, Thomas, 1814-45
Devlin, Polly, 1941-
Dillon, Eilis, 1920-94
Doyle, Roddy, 1958-
Drennan, William, 1754-1820
Dunsany, Lord, 1878-1957
Durcan, Paul, 1944-
Edgeworth, Maria, 1767-1849
Egan, Desmond, ca. 1940-
Evans, Estyn, 1905-89
Farrell, J. G., 1935-74
Ferguson, Samuel, 1810-86
Fitzmaurice, George, 1877-1963
Flanagan, Thomas, 1923-

Flower, Robin, 1881-1946
French, Percy, 1854-1920
Friel, Brian, 1929-
Gregory, Lady Augusta, 1852-1932
Hall, Mrs C. S., 1800-81
Hartnett, Michael, 1941-
Heaney, Seamus, 1939-
Hewitt, John, 1907-87
Higgins, Aidan, 1927-
Iremonger, Valentin, 1918-
Johnston, Denis, 1901-84
Johnston, Jennifer, 1930-
Joyce, James, 1882-1941
Kavanagh, Patrick, 1904-67
Keane, John B., 1928-
Keane, Molly, 1904-
Kelly, Maeve, 1930-
Kennelly, Brendan, 1936-
Kickham, Charles, 1828-82
Kilroy, Thomas, 1934-
Kinsella, Thomas, 1928-
Kiely, Benedict, 1919-
Lavin, Mary, 1912-
Le Fanu, Sheridan, 1814-73
Lever, Charles, 1806-72
Lewis, Cecil Day, 1904-72
Longford, Lady Christine, 1900-80
Lover, Samuel, 1797-1868
MacBride, Maud Gonne, 1866-1953
MacDonagh, Donagh, 1912-68
MacDonagh, Thomas, 1878-1916
Macken, Walter, 1915-67
MacLaverty, Bernard, 1942-
MacMahon, Bryan, 1909-
MacNeice, Louis, 1907-63
Mangan, James Clarence 1803-49

McGahern, John, 1934-
McGuinness, Frank, 1956-
McLaverty, Michael, 1907-1992
Molloy, M. J., 1917-94
Montague, John, 1929-
Moore, George, 1852-1933
Moore, Thomas, 1779-1852
Mulkerns, Val, 1925-
Murdoch, Iris, 1919-
Murphy, Richard, 1927-
Murphy, Tom, 1935-
O'Brien, Edna, 1930-
O'Brien, Kate, 1897-1974
O'Brien, Flann (pen-name of Brian O'Nolan), 1911-66
O'Casey, Sean, 1880-1964
O'Connor, Frank, 1903-66
O'Duffy, Eimar, 1893-1935
O'Faolain, Julia, 1932-
O'Faolain, Sean, 1900-91
O'Flaherty, Liam, 1896-84

O'Nolan, Brian, 1911-66
Paulin, Tom, 1949-
Plunkett, James, 1920-
Robinson, Lennox, 1886-1958
Ross, Martin, 1862-1915
Shaw, George Bernard, 1856-1950
Somerville, E. OE., 1858-1949
Spenser, Edmund, 1552?-99
Swift, Jonathan, 1667-1745
Synge, J. M., 1871-1909
Thackeray, William Makepeace, 1811-63
Tóibín, Colm, 1955-
Trevor, William, 1928-
Trollope, Anthony, 1815-82
Wilde, Sir William, 1815-76
White, W. J. 'Jack', 1920-80
Yeats, W. B., 1865-1939

Quotations from *The Irish Times* are from 1993-94.